PENGUIN BOOKS

THE ENTREPRENEUR'S GUIDE

Philip Holland is president and founder of the largest privately owned doughnut shop chain in America, Yum Yum Donut Shops, Inc. He divides his time between homes in Studio City and Palm Springs, California.

THE
ENTREPRENEUR'S GUIDE

How to Start and Succeed in Your Own Business

PHILIP HOLLAND

PENGUIN BOOKS

PENGUIN BOOKS
Viking Penguin Inc., 40 West 23rd Street,
New York, New York 10010, U.S.A.
Penguin Books Ltd, Harmondsworth,
Middlesex, England
Penguin Books Australia Ltd, Ringwood,
Victoria, Australia
Penguin Books Canada Limited, 2801 John Street,
Markham, Ontario, Canada L3R 1B4
Penguin Books (N.Z.) Ltd, 182–190 Wairau Road,
Auckland 10, New Zealand

First published in the United States of America by
G. P. Putnam's Sons 1984
Published in Penguin Books 1986

Copyright © Philip Holland, 1984
All rights reserved

LIBRARY OF CONGRESS CATALOGING IN PUBLICATION DATA
Holland, Philip (Philip Clark)
   The entrepreneur's guide.
   Reprint. Originally published: New York:
Putnam, c1984.
   Includes index.
   1. New business enterprises.   I. Title.
[HD62.5.H64   1986]   658.1'141   85-25811
ISBN 0 14 00.8527 0

Printed in the United States of America by
R.R. Donnelley & Sons, Harrisonburg, Virginia
Set in Times Roman

Except in the United States of America,
this book is sold subject to the condition
that it shall not, by way of trade or otherwise,
be lent, re-sold, hired out, or otherwise circulated
without the publisher's prior consent in any form of
binding or cover other than that in which it is
published and without a similar condition
including this condition being imposed
on the subsequent purchaser

ACKNOWLEDGMENTS

I am indebted to the following individuals whose confidence and efforts were so helpful. Hershey Eisenberg gave me abundant measures of encouragement that fueled my momentum and cheered me on throughout the entire writing process. Mike Love was sensitive and constructive in his appraisal of the first draft and I owe him many thanks for his comments. Vivian Davis, with her great DEC word processor, did more than process the manuscript; her suggestions and extra efforts are very much appreciated. I applaud Kathleen Marusak for her work in revision and editing, and also for her enthusiasm about the material.

I would also like to express my personal thanks to my literary agent, Jane Gelfman, of John Farquharson Ltd., who demonstrated a most fortunate combination of traits which included great professional capability and a cheerful optimism that was very reassuring to me.

Finally, it has been my good fortune to have Christine Schillig, Associate Publisher of G. P. Putnam's Sons, as my editor. I am deeply grateful to Chris for her great skill in managing the publication of this book, and especially for her tireless, expert, and honest work in line editing and editorial suggestions.

To the memory of
JAMIE
Who inspired it

And
PEGGY
Who supported it

CONTENTS

	PREFACE	11
	INTRODUCTION	17
STEP ONE:	Do I Want To Be in Business?	21
1	Stop and Think	23
2	Know Thyself	29
3	Guts, Brains, and Capital	35
4	Winning the Game	37
5	Dedication	44
6	Decide for Yourself	46
STEP TWO:	What and Where?	51
7	Do What You Like To Do	53
8	Fill a Need	61
9	Hitch Your Wagon to a Star	67
10	Specialize	75
11	Now: Decide What Business	81
STEP THREE:	Planning the Attack	85
12	Partners	87
13	Learn by Doing	98
14	Quality Without Compromise	100
15	Pilot Operation First	108

16	H.B.S., I Love You	116
17	Shall I Franchise?	119
18	Keep Score	125
19	Cash Flow	131
20	Learn from Others	141
21	Horror Story	150
22	Hit the Beaches	154
STEP FOUR:	Operations	157
23	Location, Location, Location	159
24	Your First Lease	166
25	Create Profit Centers	173
26	How To Buy	183
27	How To Borrow Money	192
28	Sales Talk	200
29	When Your Feet Are in the Fire	209
STEP FIVE:	Put It All Together	217
30	Shoemaker, Stick to Thy Last	219
31	A Pleasant Experience	225
32	Unbend the Bow	229
33	Stay Well	236
34	*Vaya con Dios*	240
	INDEX	243

PREFACE

Is anyone crazy to go into business in these times? The start-up entrepreneur in the 1980s is entering free enterprise in an extraordinary period of history. This decade could be one of worldwide hyperinflation followed by economic chaos, or a period of depression and deflation. The United States is experiencing inflation caused by uncontrollable deficit spending. At the same time, economic vitality is ebbing away as it is replaced by a highly taxed welfare state.

Actually, this may not be a bad time at all for the entrepreneur. If you are employed, you will be hurt by either inflation or deflation, but the entrepreneur can find opportunity in either. With inflation, he can borrow now and pay back with cheap dollars later on. With deflation, he can stay liquid and pick up bargains. The entrepreneur may have the best of either world . . . if he knows how to use it.

My wife and I were recently in Tahiti, at a lovely hotel owned by three Americans. One had been a lawyer, one a stock broker, and the third had been a salesman. The three decided they would rather live in Tahiti than pursue jobs in California. So they gave up careers and became farmers and later hotel operators in the South Sea Islands. They are happy in their new lives and have become successful, too.

Where we live and what we do are up to each of us. If we do not enjoy what we're doing, we should change. Perhaps moving to Tahiti is an extreme example, yet many find it difficult to change work or start a business. Any number of reasons may deter us from switching out of unrewarding work: lack of training, fear of failure, concern about supporting a family. But no matter how compelling the reasons are to stick with unhappy careers, we all have the right to change.

The idea of going into business leaves most people with a bad case of the jitters, like jumping into a murky pond to either swim or drown. This mystique of beginning a business exists because most of us haven't any idea what it will be like, and that lack of familiarity is coupled with another obstacle: fear. What we fear, of course, is that we will drown rather than swim. While business failure is always possible, keep in mind that many fail in their jobs. Any job which is not a pleasant experience is a failure, and there are surely more job failures than those experienced by persons who go into business for themselves.

Not everyone has the combination of credentials necessary to become successful in business. In fact, it is only an uncommon person who has the makeup to become an entrepreneur. Anyone who is seeking to make a change should look at the possibilities, including that of becoming an entrepreneur.

This book is a guide for potential entrepreneurs. It will tell what kind of person it takes, what planning is necessary, and what experience is required. Becoming an entrepreneur is like flying a jet plane. Even the most naturally gifted pilot must still learn the technical aspects about that jet in order to fly it.

This book will put you in touch with the crucial elements for the entrepreneur. Everything here comes from experience. I worked for a large corporation and resigned from a position of promise to start my own business. I was successful and then later was a failure. Finally, I achieved success that exceeded my greatest expectations. This book is a guide to what to do, and what not to do, when you go into business.

There is nothing better for men than that they should be happy in their work, for that is what they are here for, . . . so let them enjoy it now.

SOLOMON

It is not easy to make money.

VERNON RUDOLPH

THE ENTREPRENEUR'S GUIDE

INTRODUCTION

Sometimes big problems can be solved by breaking them down into smaller ones. Then, when each part is solved, the overall solution becomes clear, like putting together a jigsaw puzzle.

The process of becoming an entrepreneur is not a simple one. Your future and your family's future is at stake. As in problem solving, you can make your approach safer and easier by breaking up big decisions into smaller ones.

Fortunately, going into business falls neatly into a step-by-step approach. At any step along the way you can decide whether to proceed to the next one or to check out. The steps are:

1. Decide if you want to be in business.
2. Decide what business to be in, and where.
3. Prepare to start.
4. Start.
5. Make it all work.

This book is divided into sections discussing each of these steps. Each section is composed of chapters dealing with key elements to consider in that step. There is an evaluation chapter at the end of the first three steps to provide you with a framework for making your decision on the step under consideration. For example, Step One deals with the question you must answer first: "Do I want to be in business?" The chapters are subjects to be considered, and a final chapter helps you reach this decision. If your decision is yes, then you proceed to Step Two.

Step Two gives you considerations that are crucial to the next question, which is "What and where?" If there is ever a period in your life that requires thought rather than action, it is this one. Too many business owners spend unhappy and unrewarding lives because they galloped off in the wrong direction.

Step Three is called "Planning the Attack," and it shows you how to prepare for starting a business. An entrepreneur's state of readiness before starting will separate most of the winners from the losers. The winners will be the ones who proceed with all guns loaded, and a clear plan of attack.

One fact will become clear to you: going into business requires a sequential approach. The steps you take must be done in a certain order. What is the point of deciding on a business if you haven't first come to a clear conclusion that you want to be in business at all? Why devote yourself to planning for a business unless you are quite sure that it is the right one to be in? What is the sense of burning the bridges of a career and risking all that you have unless your preparations are complete?

Step Four, "Operations," is a matter of sharing operating experiences with you. Each chapter will enable you to avoid a trial-and-error approach in areas of operation that are important to maintaining equilibrium and growth. The subjects covered in "Operations" can be applied to any business. Also, they will provide you with tools that you simply will not find in textbooks.

Step Five is called "Put It All Together." One pitfall for most entrepreneurs is that we tend to become eccentric, or out of balance. Our lives become distorted because of the amount of time we put into our businesses. In many cases this leads to unhappy lives. To become successful in your own business requires careful thought and planning and work, but it is not necessary that you devote your whole life to work. To be truly successful, you will want to accomplish some broader goals. Step Five gives some tips on accomplishing these goals, and thereby shows you how to eliminate the eccentricity that is so common in business owners.

When you go into business for yourself, you will be blazing new trails in a direction that you've never tried before. What you read here are experiences along those trails that will be helpful to you. Every program described here works. While some have been found through a trial-and-error process, they all work. Some of the experiences have been gloriously rewarding. Others were horrifying. The ones that are horror stories might be most helpful, because I hope to save you a great deal of wear and tear. Starting your own business is a great adventure, and the following steps can make it safe and rewarding as well.

STEP ONE

DO I WANT TO BE IN BUSINESS?

First things first. To succeed in your own business, you must possess certain individualistic attributes. This beginning step will identify these traits and you can determine whether or not you belong to the rather uncommon, exciting world of men and women who are entrepreneurs.

1
STOP AND THINK

Anyone considering starting his own business enjoys a marvelous and paradoxical quirk of fate. The asset most valuable to this enterprise comes free of charge. It is the power to think. It is also a paradox that this key ingredient is far too often not put to use. Your greatest risk in starting a business is that you will not stop and think through certain decisions. Failures are caused by mistakes, and mistakes happen when we do not think.

There is an old German saying that reminds us: "We get too soon old and too late smart." One reason for this is that most of us are action-oriented rather than thought-oriented. If you would like to test the validity of this, think back to the three most important decisions you have ever made in your life. Would you have made better decisions had you given more thought to them than you did at the time?

The reason we are inclined to act rather than think when making important decisions is that it is easier. Mental labor is far more taxing than physical activity. It's easy to be busy; in fact, staying busy sometimes is used as a substitute for thinking. We keep so busy that we just don't have time to think.

If there is ever a time in your life when you need to stop and think and resist the natural urge to act, it is before going into business for yourself. Most really successful people are thinkers who are calculating in their decisions. The adjectives such as "shrewd," "clever," "brainy," and even "cunning," that describe successful entrepreneurs are all related to the mental activity called thinking. We win through mental efforts rather than exploits of physical skill.

What is needed, then, is a process by which you expose each of your crucial decisions to the scrutiny of thought. The purpose of this chapter will be to show you how to accomplish this. Each critical decision will be made with the discipline of a structured analysis that will force you to think.

There is a compelling reason for you to use a discipline that forces you to think: the consequences of not doing so are absurdly demoralizing. So many of us have made thoughtless decisions in our lives that have resulted in years of unhappiness or misfortune. Decisions made in the twinkling of an eye can be devastating if they concern crucial issues.

It is curious how the course of our lives is determined by a few impetuous commitments. I remember in junior high school telling a counselor that I planned to become an engineer. There was really no thinking at all behind that statement. At the time, being an engineer happened to be an acceptable career. My answer to the counselor became a goal, which became a course of study, which became a career. All without thought.

Going into your own business is like selecting a mate. You will either be fortunate and successful, or you will create your own private hell. The selection of a mate can be clouded by infatuation, and the decision to go into business can be influenced by emotional or impetuous elements.

Opening your own business can be compared with the selection of a mate in another respect. It will sometimes come naturally, as in the case of childhood sweethearts with similar backgrounds who marry, or the selection can be made by varying degrees of thoughtful consideration. Many people never really had to decide whether to be in business, because it just came naturally. I have a friend who owns a successful car dealership, and his son, who is now in college, has worked in the business ever since he was seven years old. After college, the young man wants to join his father's business. He is fortunate to have such a natural selection.

The other possibility is that a person may have the desire to be in business for himself but be at a complete loss as to which business. He must make a choice. My advice is to *stop and think*; resist the impulse to act without thought.

I had been working for a large corporation for eleven years when I decided to start my own business. I resigned from the company without having the foggiest idea of what business to engage in. That decision itself was not bad, because I had the financial capability to take whatever time was necessary.

At the time, a good friend gave me a piece of advice, which I failed to follow, and it was to *stop and think*. Specifically, the advice was to do nothing for a year except look around and study possibilities. I had saved enough money to be able to do this and still have an adequate amount for start-up capital. Unfortunately, I did not follow this advice. My problem was that I had itchy feet, and was overanxious to get started. It was far easier for me to act than to think.

One way to get ideas is to look in the "business opportunities" section of the newspaper. It happens to be an absolutely dreadful approach, which I do not recommend. However, when I started out I spent a good deal of time looking through these ads. After about three months, I ran across one in the *Los Angeles Times* by a fellow who had a company that manufactured automatic doughnut machines. He was quite a guy: an innovative inventor and a very good salesman. He was such a good salesman that he convinced me to become a partner in his small, undercapitalized company.

I will condense the next two years into a short sentence. Making the business work was like trying to straighten out a bucket of worms. All of my savings finally ended up in this company, and it was a terrifying and fatiguing experience. Finally, good fortune struck and the Pillsbury Company bought the business from the two of us.

I escaped this first experience with my investment intact and with an on-the-job course in entrepreneurship under my belt. Of course, the most important lesson was that I should have stopped and thought before ever going into it. If I had, I would have spared myself two years of pure hell.

Even when there is no question that you want to be in your own business, that you know exactly what business to be in and have credentials to do well in it, you can still get sidetracked if you don't stop and think through crucial decisions. To go ahead without preparation would be like having a trained boxer going into the ring with his right hand tied behind his back.

It is easy to say "Stop and think," but a great deal more difficult to practice it. There are forces that will interfere with your ability to think. If you understand what these deterrents are, you will be prepared to discipline your decisions. Here are some reasons why we don't want to think.

1. Impatience. Being in a hurry is a killer. Force yourself to plod through the swamps of murky, unfamiliar matters until they are clear.

2. Tunnel vision. Since we are in an increasingly specialized society, our particular work experience makes us unappreciative of other activities in the overall makeup of a business. We tend to be disdainful of the importance of unfamiliar facets.

3. Thinking is hard work. It is not even associated with pleasant experiences. However, like exercise, the more you do it the better you get at it, and the more you will enjoy it.

4. Self-confidence will short-circuit thinking. You must act as your own devil's advocate and see every side of a crucial decision. It is easier to see this flaw in others than in ourselves. Our attitude is: "You who think you know it all are very annoying to those of us who do."

5. Fear of learning what we don't want to hear will also kill thought. An entrepreneur does not have the luxury of prejudice. Every decision must withstand the harsh light of objectivity. If you have a ball painted half white and half black and you hold it up to a friend, he

might bet his house that it is black, not knowing that the side visible to you is white.

6. Although enthusiasm is an essential ingredient of starting a business, it will get in the way of calculated thought. Both are necessary, but enthusiasm must be set aside while the process of thinking takes place.

The first decision you will need to think about is whether to be in your own business at all. Next is what business to start. If you must get out of town to some hideaway in order to have time to think, then by all means do so.

There are other decisions having to do with your start-up that deserve attention. There may be the question of where you want to live. Will you be located in a place as a result of happenstance, or because you really want to be there?

If you decide to go into your own business, you will need to make decisions regarding your priorities in life. You must plan the time you wish to allocate to your family and to other activities, just as you must decide how much time you wish to spend on the business.

Each important decision can be made within a disciplined framework of scrutiny. Here is a technique you can use, putting each decision through the following five tests:

1. For a writer to achieve a daily harvest of words, he must spend a certain number of hours each day in writing. Output is proportional to time spent. This holds true in thinking about your decisions, too. Force yourself to devote a certain amount of time each day to the questions at hand.

2. Let your thoughts mature and clarify with time. The best shots are not those made from the hip, but those involving lots of time spent in sighting, calibrating, and finally slowly squeezing the trigger. So it is with your decisions. Try, even in a calculated way, to sleep on your decisions. Over a period of days or weeks, answers will surface.

3. Calculate every risk. This would particularly apply

to the initial question of what kind of a business to operate. You must calculate your exposure to loss. Risks can be calculated or they can be blind. Any enterprise involves risks, and my point is not to attempt to eliminate them, only to calculate very carefully. Expose yourself to risks in increments. Do not bet all of your available money, but only an amount you are willing to lose. The worst risk you can take is to commit all of your resources to a high-risk undertaking. This is not to say you should never commit all of your assets to a business, nor is it saying you should never take a high risk. The trick is never, never to do both at the same time. This point will be repeated later, and it cannot be repeated too often. If you learn this one rule and nothing else between these covers, you will be amply rewarded.

4. Stimulate and expand your thought by bringing other minds to bear on the question. Thoughtfully and with your whole brain tuned in on "receive," ask others for their advice on the matter. Ask your spouse. Ask the highest, most successful person in the field (whether you know him or not; you might have to introduce yourself). Ask your banker, lawyer, accountant, and any person whose mind you respect. You will be amazed how these people will "turn on" to give you their best. If the tables were turned, and a friend came to you for advice, wouldn't you respond carefully and helpfully?

5. Use a "for" and "against" list. Any important issue will clear up if you tabulate all of the points in favor and all of the points against it. The more you tabulate, the more your thoughts are stimulated. In most cases, answers will become clear as the pro and con considerations are spread out in front of you, side by side.

In summary, for each important decision:

- Spend time each day on it.
- Sleep on it.

- Calculate every risk.
- Consult others.
- Use a "for" and "against" list.

Each decision will require objectivity. Pull yourself away from the point of view that seems to dominate your mind, and act as a dispassionate judge who must weigh all of the evidence. Visualize yourself as Solomon himself, who is not swayed by the mob of unthinking zealots, but who will decide each issue only on the basis of wisdom. Visualize how your success will materialize; it will come about by the combination of your experienced skills plus the absence of mistakes. Remember the advice on how to never lose at tennis—all you must do is return every ball. In business, you return every ball by thoughtful decisions that avoid mistakes.

Calculate; weigh; balance; cogitate; contemplate; examine; research. Stop and think. Your degree of success will be proportional to the time you spend in thought.

2
KNOW THYSELF

Any old sea captain will tell you that his safe passage over the years was made possible by following "The Rules of the Road." The Rules of the Road are a set of internationally agreed-upon signals that govern passage in shipping lanes and hazards at sea. Without them, putting out to sea would be dreadfully perilous.

If you start a business of your own, you are going to be your own skipper. You will be setting out with no Rules of the Road to guide you. They will be written as you go and will develop out of experience. Any rules that you have "going in" that will help you steer away from dangers should be worth considering.

This book will share experiences that can act as Rules of the Road for you. A great number of people have gone into their own business as a result of accepting advice regarding the benefits of being your own boss. Many others have decided against starting a business because of the horrific stories they have heard. This world has a great number of people who are in their own businesses and shouldn't be, and perhaps an equal number who should be and are not.

The trick is to *know thyself* and to make up your own mind. Each chapter here describes different rules for being in your own business. You will be able to decide yourself whether the entrepreneurial game is one you want to play.

To begin, one essential ingredient must be present, and only you can decide if you have it. To identify it, let's first recite the definition of "entrepreneur," according to the Merriam-Webster dictionary: "one who organizes, owns, manages and assumes the risks of a business." The essential ingredient is to have a compelling and instinctive desire to fulfill that role. You have heard of the instinct that compels salmon to swim upstream in order to fulfill their reproductive roles. Well, entrepreneurs also have an inner desire that must be fulfilled by the role they play in assuming risks and management in a business.

Not everyone has this "entrepreneur's instinct." It is not altogether a common trait. Surely you have friends who have expressed a desire to be in their own businesses but never quite get started. These unfortunate people suffer from a curious dilemma. On the one hand, they are too unhappy in their work to want to continue, and on the other, they simply do not have the necessary impulsive instinct to operate for themselves. It reminds me of the dilemma Jack Kennedy feared about leaving the presidency. He said he was too young to retire, but not old enough to write his memoirs.

Let me give you an example of two fellows who were building careers in a large corporation. In both cases, they were considering the possibility of starting their own business. One did and one did not. Since I was one of these two fellows, this will be a firsthand case history.

After college and service in the Navy, I went to work for Johns-Manville Corporation as an industrial sales engineer. A friend of mine started to work for Johns-Manville at about the same time, in the same capacity. During our first six or seven years with the company, Hank Moreno and I each had our own sales territories and we called on a wide variety of small businesses.

Since most of our customers were small firms, we had access to their owners and to their operations. As young, aggressive salesmen, we found it an educational experience to watch these small companies. We admired the sense of proprietorship, prestige, and authority the owners enjoyed. We were aware, too, of the rewards of ownership that were evident: the personalized offices, company cars, and the independence. The owners seemed to relish their roles as presidents.

Hank and I were bitten by the idea of going into business for ourselves. We also had a specific one in mind. We decided to become a distributor of Johns-Manville products for the area we lived in. At the time there was an opening for such a distributorship, so we approached the local Johns-Manville management and made our pitch. Unknown to us, Johns-Manville already had plans for another company to take over the product lines we wanted to handle, so we were politely turned down.

Later we both accepted promotions into management jobs in the New York headquarters of the company. Even the exciting atmosphere of working and living in New York could not extinguish my inner desire to do something on my own. I had absolutely no idea what kind of business I wished to engage in. After two years in New York I finally resigned in order to return to California; I still had no idea what kind of business to start. Many of my friends thought I had suddenly gone crazy because I was on the threshold of a promising future in the company's higher echelons. In my case, for better or for worse, there was a compelling desire to be in business for myself which made my action of resigning the only course to follow.

But Hank Moreno found that the environment of a large company had the appeal and challenge to outscore his desire to be an entrepreneur. His leaning toward the corporate life was reinforced by two developments. First, he was very good at it and he could get ahead in the special environment of corporate life. He had the ability to accomplish what he described as "passing through the eye of the needle" into top management positions.

The second factor that crystallized Hank's status as a corporate man was his acceptance of a philosophy outlined by a Harvard Business School professor whom he met during a Harvard management course. The philosophy was that the greatest challenge for a young businessman was not in having his own business at all; it was in the corporate life. Corporate life, this professor believed, was the better environment: it involved the exercise of great power and access to enormous resources; it brought the benefits of vacations, stock options, large salaries, and prestige. The professor's conclusion was that the large corporation offered the greatest potential, and not the route of the entrepreneur. Hank came to agree with this belief.

Hank "knew himself," and he followed good judgment by accepting and building his corporate career rather than by making his way into entrepreneurship, for which he really did not have a compelling instinct. Our selection of different roles was based on our different instincts rather than our relative abilities.

Most people who have thought about starting their own business never actually start something of their own. We therefore tend to write them off as talkers without courage. It may be more accurate to identify them as part of that great body of people who have the dilemma of not being happy in their work but who are also frustrated by not having the entrepreneur's instinct. Rather than suffer from this unhappiness, perhaps such people should simply seek out a work-life that will be satisfying to them, without looking for the solution in their own businesses.

For those of us who, for better or worse, have this entrepreneur's instinct, this desire will get us through the first eye of our needle. It will get us started in some business of our own. Then, as in the case of the salmon whose instinct compels it to leave the sea where it has spent much of its life, we venture upstream to swim or drown. Entrepreneurs are all just the same, as the salmon are all the same. Nothing will keep us from accomplishing our role.

I have always enjoyed reading biographical books about successful people. The great artists of the world were instinctively compelled to persist in their fields of endeavor without any regard to benefits or problems. Entrepreneurs who have achieved the highest levels of success were men and women who went into business for themselves because it just came naturally, and they simply had to persist. Nothing will deter such a person. It does take more guts than brains to go into business: salmonlike, instinctive guts.

Stories of such business tycoons provide instructive reading, and I would certainly recommend biographies of Ford, Kaiser, Rockefeller, Getty, and the other giants. They all embodied certain common characteristics: natural brilliance in business, hard work, good luck, and that old standby, entrepreneurial instinct.

Let's assume you are indeed imbued with the irrepressible urge to be your own boss. If this is true, you will find yourself in an involuntary sequence of *be-do-have*. Let me explain.

Since you already have the entrepreneurial instinct, you have already started your swim upstream. Whether you are aware of it or not, you are starting at the state of being an entrepreneur. Whether you like it or not, you're at the point of *be*.

The second posture you will take after *be* is to *do*. You do it. You assume the risk and management of an enterprise of your own. If you are ten years old, this might take the form of the classic lemonade stand. If you're an adult, the progression to *do* could vary from a massive commitment of your money to a part-time garage-operated sideline. This progression from *be* to *do* is a natural one, and experiencing it is exhilarating.

The final sequence is to *have* whatever your unique combination of abilities, work, luck, and all the other variables will produce. You may not be a Rockefeller; in fact, you may not even be successful, but you will have played the game your own way.

Lots of people think about being in business, but most of them are daydreaming fantasies that lack the necessary involuntary impulses. Others are simply naturals at being their own boss. You must determine who you really are. You must strip away all the layers of insulation you have lived with and really get to know yourself. To be an entrepreneur, you must find yourself possessed with that involuntary, natural, vital, inherent, impulsive, spontaneous instinct that demands fulfillment.

So, an initial and crucial decision you must make is, just who are you? Are you really the kind of person who finds himself compelled by his instinct to fly alone; or are you more akin to Hank, who finds happiness, reward, and challenge in his company job? Give this a great deal of thought and contemplation. Know thyself. Follow your instincts.

3
GUTS, BRAINS, AND CAPITAL

To decide if you want to start your own business, you first need to know what it takes to win. In this chapter I will describe the three ingredients for success: guts, brains, and capital.

Guts, as we've already discussed, is simply the entrepreneurial instinct. You have it or you don't.

Brains can be disposed of almost as easily. As an equation, brains equals know-how in one's field plus common sense. Know-how means experience and the requirement for it can be very specialized and limited to your own field of business.

Common sense equals prudence. Time and again, it is the prudent ones who win the ball game in business. Think about people you know who have started their own businesses. Write down a list, and alongside each name, make a note of whether each person was prudent or impetuous. My list demonstrates a clear point, as will yours: prudent people finish first and impetuous people finish last or not at all. For example, it is imprudent to put all of one's savings into a high-risk venture. Common sense would not necessarily avoid taking a risk, but the risk would be handled in a calculated manner so if the worst happens, the entire fleet is not sunk.

Common sense (prudence) also guides the entrepreneur in his decisions. Every decision creates waves, and over a period of time those cumulative waves will form the structure of a business that is either healthy or unstable. So it does take brains to be successful. Know your stuff (experience) and use common sense (prudence) in making your business decisions.

The last and least important ingredient you will need in your recipe for success is *capital*. One reason that capital is less important is that it should not take very much to start up a business.

The greatest success stories are those in which start-up capital was just about zero. To start with a small stake is to increase your chances for success. Conversely, starting up with a great amount of capital can place a handicap on the prospects for success. If this sounds a bit strange, let me explain.

The fellows who do best are those who start small. They do everything themselves. The greatest investment in a new business is sweat equity. The owner learns the ropes by doing it all himself. If he is successful in this initial start-up, he is on a sound platform from which to enlarge his enterprise. Then when he expands, he does so with a clear picture of the do's and don'ts he learned by running the operation himself. No one is going to kid him, because he has laid a foundation based on his own experience.

On the other hand, if a person starts a new business with a great amount of capital, the chances are he will yield to the temptation to delegate and thereby lose his most valuable asset: the knowledge he would have gained from the experience. The owner will lack the foundation essential for growth and withstanding adversity.

Once the entrepreneur has developed his start-up operation into a profitable business and wants to expand, he may need more capital, perhaps in an amount that will dwarf his initial capitalization. However, now he has some powerful tools. He has profits that can be used, and by virtue of being successful on a small scale, he has credit. Everything is in his favor because his initial capitalization was small.

The first really large business I owned was Yum Yum Donut Shops. When I started, I had no capital at all, and that was the greatest start-up asset I had going for me. In the first store I had to do it all: baking, washing windows, mopping the floors. It was my ticket to the top in what ultimately became a large and successful chain of stores.

I did not include hard work as one of the key ingredients along with guts, brains, and capital, because it is an inherent necessity. In describing the ingredients necessary for good health, we do not include breathing; we assume it is a necessity.

Stop and take stock of the three ingredients you will need. If you have these to begin with, you have all it takes to win:

- Guts
- Brains
- Capital.

4
WINNING THE GAME

Let's forget about business for now. Instead, let's think about how games are played. In this chapter we will be looking at those who win at games. The purpose will be to find out what makes these people different. We will identify traits that winners have in common, and we will look at the price they pay in training and sacrifice.

It is worthwhile for the potential entrepreneur to know how an athlete becomes a winner. Doesn't it seem reasonable that whatever ingredients make up a champion in sports might also be utilized in becoming a champion at business? If an Olympic gold medal winner applied all of the elements that won him the medal to becoming a business winner, he would most likely be successful at that effort, too. So the purpose of this chapter will be to find out how champions win at games. You can then evaluate your own inventory of winning ingredients to determine whether you have what it takes to succeed in business.

You already are aware that winners are the exception, not the rule. For every champion, there are a host who are "almost but not quite" champions. The same is true in business. Few have the spirit for it, and of those who do, relatively few become real winners. When you realize the price winners pay for success, you may even decide that becoming a champion at business is not for you at all.

Our niece, Jeanne Haney Neville, was a member of the U.S. swimming team in the 1976 Olympic Games. The parents and swimmers who attended the Montreal event naturally had interests in common, and a group of them continued to meet socially. My wife, Peggy, and I attended a party of this group at the home of Jeanne's parents, Terry and Ellie Haney.

It was interesting to meet parents whose lives had focused on the championship athletic careers of their children. I talked to one father whose daughter had won a gold medal. He had a lifetime interest in championship sports. Years before, he had been a member of the U.S.C. basketball team whose crosstown rival was U.C.L.A., coached at the time by John Wooden.

John Wooden accomplished one of the most incredible win–loss records in history. For the years he coached at U.C.L.A., the school was practically unbeatable. The father of the gold medal swimmer who had played against Wooden teams was a man who was very keen about winning, too. I asked him just what it was that made John Wooden so successful. The answers came out clearly and without hesitation. There were four things that made Wooden successful.

First, he knew the game. He was expert in basketball, and he knew every trick about strategy. He was totally familiar with the field he coached.

Second, he drew a very clear line in one matter, and he never crossed over that line, existing only on one side of it.

One side was win and the other was lose. He never considered any other possibility than winning the game. To lose was not a part of his thoughts, expressions, or experience.

Third, John Wooden insisted that all the players on his team conform to his standards. If any player, regardless of his ability, deviated from the Wooden standard of conduct or performance, he was immediately pulled out of the game. Even the famous Lew Alcindor (now Kareem Abdul-Jabbar) was taken out if he deviated from Wooden's standards of play.

Last, Wooden never changed the style of his game. If the team was behind with only sixty seconds left to play, it stuck to the formula. When in difficulty, other teams switched to different styles of play to break their bad luck. Wooden never did. He had developed a method of play that worked and he stayed with it through thick and thin. He always won the game.

Now, if the rules of winning games can be applied to business, John Wooden's rules would teach us some interesting guidelines. First, know the game. Know more about your own business than anybody. This comes from experiencing it (before starting on your own), and also by acquiring every bit of knowledge that is available about your field of business.

Second, play to win. This is a state of mind; your affirmative attitude will prevail in every action and decision. The goal of success is always in mind.

Third, insist that your players conform to your own high standards of conduct and performance, and if they do not, pull them out of the game. Never be satisfied with incompetent or unethical relationships with employees, suppliers, or any other business associates. If someone on your business team does not meet your standards, do as John Wooden did with his players: pull him out of the game.

Finally, stick with your game plan. Through good times and even when you are behind, stick to your own operational know-how and standards.

If you look at other great coaches, you will see the story of John Wooden repeated. They all seem to exude the same vibrations:

- An intense desire and need to win.
- An ability to motivate and inspire their players.
- A knack of orchestrating great individual performances into a smooth harmonious team, where the collective desire to win becomes an incredible and overpowering force.
- Good coaches are good recruiters. They have the ability to pick out the most promising players, and sell them on joining the team.

While winning coaches have one set of traits in common, champion athletes have another set of characteristics that set them apart. These winning athletic traits fall into the following categories.

1. Natural ability, which includes:
- Energy.
- Love of the sport. In many cases there is an instinctive affinity between a champion and his event.
- Appropriate physical characteristics. There would be no point for a jockey-sized athlete to try to excel at basketball. Physical characteristics must be appropriate for the sport, and in the case of champions, superbly appropriate.

2. Learning ability includes the following characteristics:
- Intelligence. Different sports may take different levels of intelligence. Winners must have knowledge of their event, and make optimum use of that knowledge in the game.
- Willingness to follow instructions. Champion athletes learn from champion coaches, and must be eager to follow prescribed protocols.

3. Training separates a great many athletes with natural ability from champions because of:
- Dedication. Quite aside from natural ability and learning ability, champions must experience superhuman training efforts. Every activity has its own training rules that must be satisfied in order to achieve championship. It can be extremely hard work.
- Discipline. Training requires discipline. The athlete must discipline every other aspect of his life to support his goal. He must be disciplined in his diet, his rest, and in moderating any activities that would impair his training effort.

4. Desire to win is the final cornerstone of the champion athlete:
- Winners are extraordinarily competitive. While he held the world marathon record, Derek Clayton was never shy about grinding other runners into the ground. He felt that he "trained so bloody hard" he had the right to win. Champions enjoy and thrive on competition.
- Winners have a unique success-oriented philosophy in which winning is the all-important goal.

These four cornerstones apply to any field of athletic competition, even though different sports will have different emphases. In each and every sport it takes:

1. Natural ability.
2. Learning ability.
3. Training ability.
4. The desire to win.

The same set of rules will determine champions in business. This means you can evaluate your abilities to see if you have the ingredients to win at business by scoring each of these areas:

	Your self-analysis of entrepreneurial traits. (Score yourself from 1 to 10.)
NATURAL ABILITY	
Energy	_____
Love of the sport (to be in business)	_____
Appropriate personal characteristics	_____
LEARNING ABILITY	
Intelligence	_____
Willingness to learn (before starting)	_____
TRAINING ABILITY	
Dedication	_____
Discipline	_____
THE DESIRE TO WIN	
Competitive in nature	_____
Winner's attitude	_____

Total score = _____

Total average score (divide by 9) = _____

The businessman who falls short in one or more critical areas outlined here didn't do anything wrong, he just didn't have those four basic cornerstones covered as well as the winner did.

Some champions keep their titles for many years, sustaining their careers for incredibly long periods of time. All athletes who enjoy long careers also have special traits that keep them going. Obviously they have great endurance, which over many years requires unremitting dedication to physical conditioning. These champions could not possibly enjoy years of success without paying a price in discipline, moderation, and self-sacrifice.

The same is true of successful businessmen. The ones who

build and preserve success are those who can maintain their condition by paying the same price: discipline, moderation, and self-sacrifice.

A number of interesting conclusions can be drawn from applying the traits of sports champions to starting a business. First, being in business is not at all unlike a game. The hard work, the challenge, the rewards, the penalties all fall into a competitive perspective.

Another thing becomes clear about becoming a champion: no one can give it to you and you surely can't buy it. You must do it yourself. This is also true in business.

In sports, as in business, not everyone is a winner. The reason is that winners do things that losers don't like to do: not everyone is willing to pay the price. How many thirteen-year-old girls will get up at 4:30 in the morning to swim and lift weights for five hours a day? Not many, but Olympic champions do. Indeed, they must adhere to these disciplines for years in order to win that medal.

Our increasingly socialized and sedentary society makes us more dependent on outside forces to shape our lives. As we become lazier, we find it harder to do the things that winners must do. Winning is not for everybody; only a handful of dedicated people are willing to pay the price.

Most of us prefer the easy path, so the world is full of those who "almost, but not quite" make it. Winners, on the other hand, achieve a high quality out of life. It is an individual choice.

5
DEDICATION

Dedication is a trait that successful people have in common. Since your goal in business is to be successful, it is well worth becoming familiar with the nature of dedication.

I have a friend who opened an independent doughnut shop at a certain location. I had previously turned down the spot for one of my own shops, for ample reasons. It was located in an area that summed up all of the adverse criteria for our kind of business. My friend confirmed my judgment when his store opened at the very low sales level of $1500 per week. It was a disaster.

I happened to be passing through this desolate area about a year after my friend opened his shop and was curious about how he was doing. In fact, I wondered if he was still there at all. Well, the store was open and it looked beautiful. My friend was full of smiles. During breakfast he told me his sales were now $4000 per week. I knew he was telling the truth because I could see the activity in the store, and I was overwhelmed by what he had done.

I asked my friend how he had accomplished this remarkable success. His answer was one word: "Dedication." He knew it would take product quality, cleanliness, and all of the other elements necessary for success. He dedicated himself to achieving those elements, and the store improved. The improvement fueled his dedication even further, and like a virus it infected his employees too. They also became dedicated to their jobs, and the operation continued to grow into a fantastic store within a period of one year.

A business owner is in a good position to benefit from dedication. If he succeeds, he reaps the harvest for himself. Also, his own assets are invested in the enterprise, and that motivates him too.

If dedication is to be effective, you must know your business before you start. Every business requires that certain things be accomplished if it is to succeed, and dedication means accomplishing all of them, without compromise. Dedication is the sum of knowledge and work. It is knowing what has to be done, and doing it. My friend who opened the doughnut shop knew, before he opened, exactly what had to be accomplished to make his shop work. He then saw to it that all of those things were accomplished without compromise.

When I first started in business for myself, like a fool I bought into a business that I knew nothing about. There was no way for me to begin with dedication because I did not know what to do or where to start. I had to learn the business and what had to be done to make it work. Dedication emerged only after I had become familiar with it. Once a person achieves dedication in a business objective, it is then easy to stick to his gut judgments and not be swayed or discouraged.

The lesson is: don't start a business without knowledge. Know what it takes before starting; then when you do jump in, your knowledge coupled with dedication becomes a very strong force. Never start up the business unless you have experienced all aspects of its operation. Then start with dedication.

The key ingredient of dedication is hard work, but it must be examined carefully as a tool for success. There is the story about the man who was told that if he worked the very hardest he could, he would become rich. The hardest work he knew was digging holes, so he set about digging holes in his back yard. He didn't get rich; he only got a backache. He worked hard, but without any purpose.

That may sound like a preposterous story, but it can be surprisingly near the truth in a great number of case histories of start-up entrepreneurs. I remember for many years being just like that hole digger. I earnestly believed that success was somehow related to the number of hours of digging each week. Every week I kept a mental tally of how many hours I worked. Fewer than sixty hours gave me guilt feelings. The more hours put in, the better week I had. This was all pure foolishness.

So it is easy for an entrepreneur to become eccentric about the number of hours that he works. It is not very smart. I was putting in hours rather than achieving goals. Had I been dedicated in an intelligent way, my dedication would have been identified with results rather than with the number of hours worked.

Presently I am accomplishing goals that I had not even dreamed of and am doing it in a five-day work week. I am dedicated, happy, and feeling good about work. My goal-oriented dedication, operating within a controlled time period, accomplishes much, much more than any person who is not dedicated could hope to achieve.

Most people don't have to be dedicated to earn a living. In some lines of work they don't even have to be competent. The reverse is true if you start your own business. You *must* be competent and dedicated to win.

Your sense of dedication therefore comes under scrutiny. It becomes a factor in your "first things first" decision about whether or not to be in business for yourself.

6
DECIDE FOR YOURSELF

This chapter summarizes what you need to be in business for yourself. Not many of us are fortunate in having an easy answer to this first crucial question. The reason is that we haven't had experience in knowing what it takes. We therefore tend to leap into or shun an entrepreneurial experience for impulsive and emotional reasons, without an objective analysis of our credentials.

Fortunately there are specific, basic traits that are common to the successful entrepreneur, and their absence forebodes trouble for someone deciding whether or not to start up a business. Without a sufficient quotient of entrepreneurial traits the experience can be miserable and terrifying for the entrepreneur and everyone around him, including his family. And if he can't put his finger on the missing elements, he may not know when to quit; this persistence can lead to a lifetime of frustration, unhappiness, and failure.

On the other hand, someone with a high level of entrepreneurial instincts may experience entirely different frustrations while working for others, feeling like a fish out of water until his role in life is fulfilled by starting a business on his own.

So before you even think about what business to be in, determine if you have the entrepreneur's equipment. Here are the necessary traits:

1. An entrepreneur is a thinking, calculating person, rather than one who makes decisions based on emotional considerations.
2. An entrepreneur possesses a certain instinct that can be measured but not implanted.
3. He has guts, brains, and capital, as defined previously.
4. Entrepreneurship requires a need to win.
5. An entrepreneur must have dedication.

Fortunately, you can evaluate your own traits in a very objective way. The previous five chapters will be your yardsticks. Go back to each and evaluate yourself with respect to each subject. Take Chapter 1, "Stop and Think," as an example. Does the concept of a structured, calculated approach seem appropriate for your personality? Or does it seem unessential? For Chapter 5, "Dedication," do you accept its message or does it seem superfluous?

To the extent your approach and attitudes conform to the statements in each of the five chapters, give yourself a high score. Conversely, if you honestly do not possess the characteristics, give yourself a low score. Perhaps the summation that follows will help you decide if you have the traits of an entrepreneur.

TRAITS OF A SUCCESSFUL ENTREPRENEUR
A tabulation of characteristics in Step One:
"Do I Want To Be in Business?"

CHAPTER	CHARACTERISTIC	SCORE 1-10
1. Stop and think	Thoughtful in decisions.	10
	Patient in decisions.	9
	Calculates risks carefully.	9
	Willing to get advice.	8
	Uses "for" and "against" lists.	7
2. Know thyself	Has entrepreneur's instinct.	7
	Believes in *be-do-have*.	7
3. Guts, brains, and capital	High common sense (prudence) quotient.	8
	Will use sweat equity as start-up capital.	5
4. Winning the game	High overall score on *winning traits*.	7
5. Dedication	Willingness to learn business before starting.	8
	Positive attitude regarding goal-oriented hard work.	8

In your self-analysis of entrepreneurial traits, I suggest you use a "for" and "against" list whenever you have an important decision to make. In many cases, when the facts are listed pro and con, doubts will clear up. Here is an example of such a list for the first question of the preceding tabulation, "Are you thoughtful in decisions?"

For	Against
1. Was careful in buying a house (took one year looking).	1. Bought a car without shopping around.
2. Consulted school counselor before deciding on major.	2. Got married by eloping to Las Vegas.
3. Took a course in decorating before fixing up my house.	3. Like to play "chicken" with my car.

Now, is it apparent that the items under "for" describe a different person than do those listed under "against"? In our own list, you will quickly detect how you score on this characteristic.

From your overall evaluation you may come to the conclusion not to start your own business at all. Running a business is a different way of life from working for someone. There are "different strokes for different folks" and now is your moment of truth in deciding just what kind of person you are. Either way, you're okay, provided your decision is thoughtful and objective.

Of one hundred persons who face this first decision, perhaps 10 percent have an irrepressible, compulsive desire to be in their own business. For these persons, the decision need not be made at all, because nothing could keep them away. Perhaps another 10 percent will be on the other end of the spectrum; those who can readily acknowledge that their makeup is entirely inappropriate for the role of entrepreneur. It is the 80 percent in the middle who must carefully decide whether or not going into business is the right thing to do.

If you are not ready to decide, continue reading through the next steps. Your perspective will broaden and that will help clarify this first pivotal question. Keep in mind the importance of making crucial decisions in the right sequence: First, decide if you want to be in business. Then decide what and where.

In this book I often refer to business as a game. If you are playing tennis and you lose, all you have lost is the score. If you lose in business, it is another matter entirely. Business failure is one of the ultimate forms of shame in today's world, so you want to be sure. If you decide to start a business you have a serious responsibility to win and not to lose. The next step will show you how to select a business once you have decided to become an entrepreneur.

STEP TWO

WHAT AND WHERE?

If you have what it takes to become an entrepreneur, you must make some career choices that will take clear thinking and can make the difference between a rewarding life or a self-created hell.

7

DO WHAT YOU LIKE TO DO

Since we spend most of our lives working, we might as well like what we do for a living. And if we like what we do, the chances are we will also be good at it. Liking your work should therefore become one of your basic goals. This chapter will provide some techniques to help determine the kind of work you should consider, with the goal of getting into a field you really enjoy.

As an introduction to this subject, there is a book on philosophy that I recommend. It offers the most comprehensive analysis of life I have ever read. Now, if reading philosophy bores you, this book won't, because it is only twelve pages long. Its author has an impressive reputation. In fact, he was said to be the wisest person who ever lived. His name was Solomon and the book, Ecclesiastes, may be in your house.

In his book, Solomon described his attempts to achieve happiness. He tried everything: booze, womanizing, good works, laughter, and concluded that in his rich and powerful life, his greatest source of pleasure was the joy he found in work.

Our lives are dominated by work. It can become the greatest source of happiness in life or through it we can create our own private hell. Sigmund Freud reached a conclusion similar to Solomon's. He finally decided there were two elements to a happy life: love and work. If you are considering starting a business of your own, you should surely find something you really like to do.

To decide on a field of work you enjoy, use the principle of *stop and think*. You might want to get out of town for a month and hole up where you can remove the facade that you project when you are with others. Then, honestly and analytically decide what work you would really like to do. It will take guts and imagination to identify things you like, and then figure out how you can apply them in a particular business.

Some of the possibilities that occur to you may be completely different from what you've been doing, because many of us have found ourselves in jobs or careers that we don't like. There are many haphazard, ridiculous reasons that we choose inappropriate work: usually because we have not first thought out what we like to do.

I have a friend who for years has been skipping from one business to another. I don't think he has even lasted more than five years in any one. In each case, he started a business because of a chance encounter, and it probably never occurred to him that he should make up his mind to work at something he really liked.

To set your thinking straight, let's look at some case histories of people who have succeeded in working at what they like to do.

Frank Milne is a friend I've known for twenty-five years. He loves cars, loves to sell, and loves to manage and motivate others. He now owns his own car agency.

Lloyd Rhodes is my travel agent. He loves to travel and to write about his journeys. Why shouldn't he be a travel agent?

Dallas Rytich was a shop manager in one of our Yum Yum Donut Shops, and a good one. What he especially liked to do, however, was drive. So he took special lessons, gave up his store, and is driving one of our big tractor trailer rigs. He is doing what he likes to do.

Albert Schweitzer did what he liked to do: help others. He could have enjoyed a genteel life in Europe as an applauded and respected musician, but what he wanted was to spend his life in some kind of work that would help others. So he studied to become a doctor and spent his life in Africa doing what he loved.

Many times a business will develop out of an activity that started as a hobby. Hobbies are fun, and if that activity can become a business, wonderful! I know a couple who for years made fruitcake for their friends at Christmas. It was good cake and they enjoyed making it so much that it eventually developed into a large and successful business.

Here is a technique that will stimulate thoughtful analysis so that when you pick a business it will be one you like. First, you will need a board about 3 feet by 4 feet in size. A child's chalkboard will be fine. Also, you will need a supply of 3- by 5-inch cards. The board will be used as a surface to tape up each card and, I hope, you will be filling it up with quite a number of them. You can pull up a chair next to your board and add thoughts as they come to mind, on the appropriate cards. Use Scotch tape to fasten the cards to the board. Divide the board into four sections with the following headings:

FAVORITE-ACTIVITY CARDS	FAVORITE-SENSES CARDS
SERVE-PEOPLE CARDS	COUPLING CARDS

Start by making a list of all of the activities you enjoy in your life. Be honest with yourself, and let your mind expand to include all pleasurable experiences. List each one of these favorite activities at the top of a 3×5 card.

Next, on each card make a list of all the businesses you can imagine that would relate to the pleasurable activity. Tape each card under the section of board titled "favorite-activity cards." Here is an example of what a typical favorite-activity card might look like:

I LOVE TO RUN (JOG)

Operate a runner's equipment store.
Operate a racquetball club.
Manufacture treadmills.
Manufacture running shoes.
Manufacture electronic pulse meters.
Publish a newsletter for runners.
Operate a car parking service (may be silly,
 but put it down anyway).

This particular card may not sprout a worthwhile idea, but you will never know unless you carefully consider the subject. If you love jogging as I do, it may not at first seem to be an activity at which you could make a living. On the other hand, you may be looking at something that has an enormous potential, if there are a large number of people who have needs to fill in that activity.

Now, make another set of cards for the favorite-senses section of the board, one card for each of the five senses: sight, sound, touch, smell, and taste. On these cards, list on the left side your favorite ways to enjoy each sense. Then, for each favorite enjoyment, list any possible businesses that would enable you to experience that sensual pleasure. Here is an example of a favorite-senses card:

```
                    SOUND (HEARING)

    Love music.    1. Open music store.
                   2. Start a band.
                   3. Teach music.

    Love sound     1. Operate waterfront cafe.
    of ocean.      2. Be a beachcomber.
                   3. Be a professional fisherman.

    Love silence   1. Start a mail order business.
    and quiet.     2. Become a dentist.
                   3. Be a professional writer.
```

Tape the five sense cards under this heading on your board.

Next we will go to the serve-people section. When you think about it, one of our greatest sources of pleasure is helping other people. This can therefore become a guideline in seeking out a business. If you want pleasure in your business, then start one that helps others. The next group of cards will list the ways you like to help people, to see if a business you would enjoy can be identified. Prepare each serve-people card with a heading of how you enjoy helping people, and then list specific businesses that would be appropriate under that theme. Let's assume you like to help people through religious activities. This serve-people card might say:

```
              RELIGIOUS INVOLVEMENT


       1. Open a religious bookstore.
       2. Start a youth-counseling service.
       3. Operate a mortuary.
```

As another example, let's assume you enjoy serving people by helping them physically. Such a serve-people card might look like this:

HELP PEOPLE PHYSICALLY

1. Operate a nursing home.
2. Open a weight reduction salon or gym.
3. Become a hairdresser.
4. Operate a course in how to stop smoking.
5. Operate an alcoholism rehabilitation clinic.

Finally, do some coupling to see what else comes up as a business activity you would enjoy. Many of our interests are unrelated; for example, we like cars and we like to sell. So in coupling, we use the formula, $x + y = z$. The x is one thing we like to do, y is another, possibly unrelated thing we like to do, and z is a business that could result when you combine x and y. In this example, x is a love of cars and y is a love of selling. The z becomes obvious: you would enjoy selling cars.

Now, in a new series of cards, you can begin combining x's and y's. Use all three groups of cards to think up combinations: favorite activities, favorite senses, and serve-people cards. For example, one activity card may state that you like to work with your hands, and another says that you collect clocks. So here $x + y =$ a business of repairing clocks, both out of the favorite-activity section of your board.

Remember that in coupling you are going to combine cards to see which opportunities might appear. For example, let's say that two "likes" are "like the outdoors" (sense card) and "like to climb" (activity card). Okay, now think of as many businesses as you can that would combine these two likes, such as becoming a mountain guide. This might seem impractical, but it illustrates the point! So your final step is to prepare cards that combine unrelated activities as the heading, and then see what you can develop as businesses that would use the combination to advantage. Here are some examples:

1. Love to build + love to design houses = be a speculative builder.
2. Love children + love to teach = open a nursery school.
3. Love to bake + love cheesecake = manufacture cheesecake.

The following illustration shows a sample board after cards from all four groups have been developed. You can spend a great deal of creative and productive time with your board to zero in on a worthwhile, happy business.

There is no well-known guide available to answer the simple question: To what work should I devote my life? A very few of us have some inner sense that provides an answer, but the vast majority do not have such a guiding light. Most people are engaged in their work as a result of chance.

The majority of people, then, are committed to work unrelated to their optimum abilities or preferences. Perhaps the cards you prepare will uncover a business you would enjoy operating. If you are one of the lucky few who already have made a clear choice of a business, so much the better. If you need to calculate the right answers, then the cards can be a useful tool in making a decision.

Of one thing you can be sure. People who are doing what they like to do are good at it and they relish it. Going to work is a challenge and a joy. Get in on their good thing. There is a popular beer advertisement that reminds us we have only one time around the track of life and therefore we might just as well enjoy the best. Decide what you like to do and work in that field. Everyone does well in what he or she likes to do, and it is the difference between a lifetime of fun or one of drudgery.

A final advantage in doing what you like is that you will

FAVORITE-ACTIVITY CARDS

Sample card:

> **Love Cars.**
> 1. Start an auto repair shop.
> 2. Rebuild antique cars.
> 3. Start a car leasing company.
> 4. Own a car dealership.

SERVE-PEOPLE CARDS

Sample card:

> **Love to Feed People.**
> 1. Open a restaurant.
> 2. Start a winery.
> 3. Manufacture food products.

FAVORITE-SENSES CARDS

Sight	Sound	Touch
Taste	Smell	

COUPLING CARDS
$(x + y = z)$

Sample card:

> x = like the outdoors (from senses card)
> plus y = like to climb (from activity card)
>
> equals z:
> 1. Mountain guide.
> 2. Steeplejack.
> 3. Forest ranger.

stick with it through the critical ups and downs of starting a business. You will stay with someone you love in spite of hardships. The same is true of a business.

8
FILL A NEED

Once you have made up your mind to go into a business, and have chosen something you like to do, the next step is to find a need to fill.

No business can work if it does not fill a need, but unfortunately this basic fact is devilishly easy to overlook. A start-up entrepreneur can become so enthused about an idea for a product or service that he overlooks this basic requirement. I know of a wealthy, retired businessman who lost a surprisingly large sum of money trying to sell a unique kite. He was captivated by a novel design that he felt would take hold like another Frisbee. Judging from his total flop, the problem was simply that he went into business to sell a product nobody wanted.

I recently saw a restaurant in San Jose, California, whose signs proclaimed that their specialty was artichoke dishes. They had to be kidding! The restaurant happened to be out of business, and surely the reason was that there just cannot be much of a demand for such a specialty.

Someone recently started a chain of franchised stores that specializes in selling soda pop: that's *all* they sell! The stores have a large assortment of flavors and interesting inducements to purchase soda by the case. However, it seems unlikely that they can compete with supermarkets, which offer a complete variety of these products. The overhead costs of a store selling only soda pop are going to eat them up alive, while the supermarket spreads its costs over an enormous volume of sales. Somebody overlooked the simple criterion of "fill a need."

In looking at businesses that fail, one finds that a common characteristic tends to emerge. The owner's confidence in his product or service has motivated him into business, and considerations that require critical, objective answers are overlooked. As in a football game, enthusiasm is an important ingredient, but to win you must understand the basics of the game too.

The simple question "Who wants it?" can easily be answered by observing how well existing businesses are doing. If you have a business in mind that has no competition at all, you must be especially cautious. You might find yourself in a business not only without competition but also without customers. The man who started a kite factory paid a rather high price to find this out.

Some businesses meet stable needs and others sell to customers who could do without the product or service. Filling a basic need, such as auto or shoe repair, offers the advantage of greater stability during times when consumers cannot afford the better things of life. Indeed, these businesses get better when times get tough, because then we are more inclined to have our shoes repaired than buy new ones. The doughnut business gets better in hard times. Instead of steak and eggs for breakfast, we will have a doughnut and coffee.

Basic needs, however, are stable in nature rather than expanding. Businesses that service expanding needs tend to be more exciting. In La Canada, California, there is one business that has grown more than any other in town, and its name will explain why: Sports Chalet. It is a growing operation because people are spending more money on sports and leisure activities.

Existing competition will have an important bearing on whether you will have enough customers. Has competition already satisfied the need? I would say that, with few exceptions, there is always room for another competitor, provided you keep one point clearly in mind. Be careful where you operate. Some ponds are better to fish in than others, so it would be foolish to take your pole to a small pond with few fish and many fishermen if there is a better one down the road a way.

Competition is a healthy fact of life in a free society. You must carve out your niche where the need for your product is sufficient to produce success. In Yum Yum Donuts, we open new shops every month. They are all essentially the same size and style, but our opening sales can vary enormously. In each location there must therefore be great differences in need for our products. This variation in demand is due to many reasons, but one dominating factor is competition.

We have learned that it doesn't make sense for us to put a Yum Yum Donut Shop across the street from a competitor if there is an equally good site down the road a couple of miles. It is a large world and there are lots of ponds to fish in. I have seen far too many competent operators go down the tubes because their self-confidence preempted the basic wisdom of locating in an area where demand will be the greatest.

Let's use a hypothetical case history. Say you have learned how to be an expert shoe repairman, and you wish to have the independence and satisfaction of your own business. You live in town A of 5000 population and there are three existing shoe repair services in town. Ten miles away, in town B, the population is 15,000 and there is only one existing shoe repair service. Question: Where will you best fill a need? Certainly common sense tells you to go to town B.

This example tells you something else too. You should go out and seek the best pond as part of your planning phase before going into business. If you did not take this attitude, you would simply open your shop in town A. In doing so, you might have made a fateful mistake that could have been easily avoided. Filling a need therefore also requires that you seek out the best marketplace in which to do business.

The kind of need that you fill will determine whether you

will have a big business or a small one. If the demand for what you sell is widespread, where people everywhere can use your product or service, then you will have a potentially big business. On the other hand, if you fill a local need you will have a small one.

Let's look at some examples of local needs that would be served by small businesses. If you opened a dog-grooming parlor, surely your services would be localized. The same would hold true for a dry-cleaning shop, gift shop, or flower shop. Any activity in which multiplication of your individual capability is either difficult or impossible will result in a localized and therefore limited business.

On the other hand, if you are interested in a big business, people everywhere must benefit. Remember that the world is densely populated and highly developed today. Products which in themselves seem insignificant can become the beginning of giant firms serving enormous markets. Some years ago a man had a hearing aid in which a miniature connection to the batteries kept breaking. He learned that others with hearing aids also had the same trouble, so he invented a new miniature connection that solved the problem. There was a widespread need for that connector and it was soon used everywhere in all sorts of applications. The company that grew out of that one simple device, Microdot, has become a large and successful business.

In most cases when people strike it rich in business, they have hit a perfect bull's-eye in filling a need. If you think at random of the greatest success stories in modern business, invariably the reason is satisfaction of a widespread demand. Ford, Xerox, and Rockefeller all hit bull's-eyes. The more widespread the clamor for the product, the more spectacular were the products.

This essential ingredient that makes some strike it rich is also a double-edged sword. If a business is conceived and absolutely misses the target of filling a need, no matter what guts, brains, capital, or effort is put forth, the result will be disaster. A business that does not satisfy a need cannot work.

Filling a need can be a function of time. A product that might do well at one period can be made obsolete by technology. This is covered in the next chapter, "Hitch Your Wagon to a Star." The trick is to plan for a business whose product or service satisfies a present and, ideally, future need as well.

The town or city also must be considered, since a business can do marvelously well in one location and fail miserably in another. A doughnut shop in a new suburban community with lots of young families will probably do well. That same shop in Beverly Hills would be a disaster. The first location fills a need because children and young working parents are prime customers. The Beverly Hills location would not fill a need because older, affluent, weight-conscious people are simply not doughnut eaters.

Let's look at some examples of needs.

1. In an area where there are young families and lots of children:
   a. Toy store
   b. Children's clothing store
   c. Fast-food operation
   d. Nursery

2. In an affluent area:
   a. Antique shop
   b. Expensive gift shop
   c. Pet store
   d. Health gym

3. In a retirement area:
   a. Bookstore
   b. Health needs
   c. Hobby shop

4. In a poor area:
   a. Secondhand store
   b. Auto repair shop
   c. Appliance repair shop

You should begin to catch the drift that a business must fill needs appropriate to the area in which it is located. Each business must be checked with respect to the question: "Where are enough people who want what I intend to sell?" Potential businesses that intrigue may disappear from your mind after this scrutiny.

Here are some questions to ask yourself in order to tell if a business will fill a need:

1. Have competitors already proven the existence of a demand?
2. Have you clearly defined in your own mind who needs your product?
3. Have you defined the optimum market for your product as to economic, ethnic, and age considerations?
4. Is the need now being filled poorly, and if so, could you do a far better job?
5. Does the *need* already exist, or is it *your concept* of what people need?
6. Can you benefit from available statistics such as population, average income, traffic patterns, etc.?

The worst possible conclusion you may reach is that, within the area where you wish to live, the need you want to fill has already been fully satisfied by others. It is far better, however, to reach this conclusion before starting up than to learn it through experience.

You can visualize, then, that to fill a healthy demand becomes one of the basic qualifiers to consider before you start. If you are planning to engage in something you are especially fond of, it becomes critically important to be sure about this.

Your process of deciding on a business now has an additional guideline in your plan of action. Whatever you do must be something that fills a need.

9
HITCH YOUR WAGON TO A STAR

The first step in deciding on a business was to do what you like to do. The second step was to fill a need. This chapter will review the importance of getting into a business at the right time. Sometimes it seems that certain people have an easy time in making a business work, while others struggle valiantly without much success at all. The chances are that the person with the easy time is in a business that is experiencing growth, so you should understand the importance of hitching your business wagon to a rising star.

Fifteen years ago a friend of mine went into the business of direct selling of a photo album plan. For the first few years his business grew and prospered. Then, some years later, his sales began to drift downward. No matter what he did or how hard he worked, sales continued to drop. Today he is doing about one-half the volume he did years ago. His ability to operate the business hasn't diminished; in fact, the longer he is in it the better he gets. He is still working as hard as he always has. What do you think changed?

The normal life-span of his business, which could have gone on for many years, was drastically foreshortened by outside forces, in the form of new laws. One of these laws provided a cooling-off period during which time a buyer could reconsider and cancel a purchase made under the spell of a direct salesman. So a sale is not really made until the cooling-off period has elapsed without the buyer's changing his mind.

While this law is commendable for consumer protection, it was hurtful to my friend's business. As you can imagine, it was difficult to get good direct salesmen to work under such a handicap. My friend's business entered a declining phase of its life-span.

We have a fairly good idea of our own life-span possibilities. We know, too, that different forms of living species all have widely individualistic life expectancies. I would like you to apply this thought to business, because different enterprises have their own life-span too. Any business has a life-span that starts at its creation, grows, matures, declines, and finally dies.

Let's look at the Hula Hoop. This business had a life-span of about six months. You might say this would not offer the greatest possibility as a business because it is not likely to be around very long.

Next, let's look at the manufacturing of steam locomotives. Here was a business that had a moderately good life-span of perhaps one hundred years. But over a period of time, this business declined and finally died too. During the growth period, steam locomotives offered great opportunities, but you wouldn't have been thrilled to be in it during its decline, when diesel locomotives took over.

Finally, consider the grocery store. In this business, one problem you need not face would be its business life cycle.

The life-span of a business forms a curve something like this:

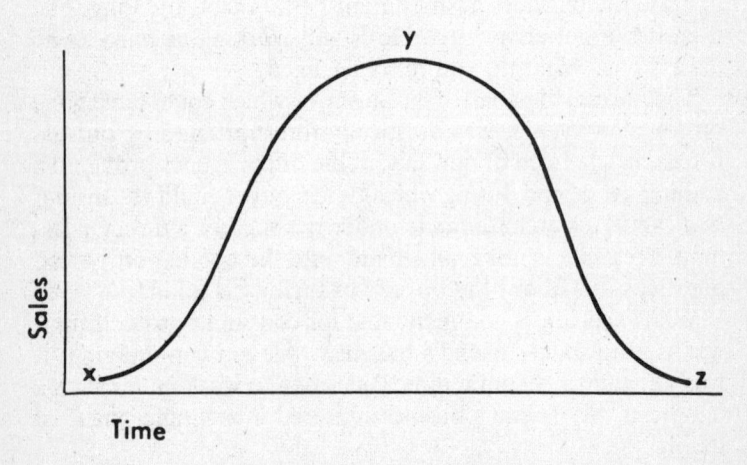

Life-span Curve of a Business

X is the point in time when a business starts, at zero sales. Y indicates the point at which it reaches its optimum level of sales. Z is the termination of the business. The growth part of the sales curve between x and y begins at a slow rate, builds up to a faster rate as the curve steepens upward, and then diminishes to zero after the peak is reached. The down side of the life-span curve, from y to z, starts with a slow rate of drop, accelerates downward at a high rate of decline, and then tapers off into oblivion.

The interval of time between x and z will vary depending on the life-span. In the case of the Hula Hoop, the interval was six months; for the steam locomotives it was one hundred years. The grocery store will face considerable risk from competition, but it does not have a life-span problem because it fills an ongoing need. The trick is to carefully select a business that still has future growth and to avoid those that are on the down side of this roller coaster curve. Best of all is to "get in on the ground floor," at the very beginning of the curve.

Perhaps you want to be in your own business but still don't know what kind. In one way, this is an advantageous starting point. You are not committed to a venture that isn't at a favorable position on the curve. If you are starting without a business in mind, you might just as well hitch your wagon to a star.

In deciding on a business, each of us will begin from a different starting point. You may already have had experience in something and this becomes a natural selection. If so, verify the curve of that business.

If you have no idea what type of business to start, you are not facing bad luck at all. You have the freedom to calculate before you choose. You can look at any number of possibilities and evaluate each one on the basis of whether it is on the growth part of its life-span or whether it is declining.

In hitching your wagon to a star, there are a few points to keep in mind. First, do not confuse the overall life-span of a business with its ups and downs. While our own lives have a span of, let us say, 75 years, there are many ups and downs we experience within that overall period. You must have the perception to distinguish between the absolute, overall life-span of a business and the ups and downs that take place.

One example might be investment banking, a business that can go into long periods of slump when customers lose their interest in common stocks. This does not mean, however, that investment banking is in the declining phase of its existence. It is part of the cyclical swing between sunny and rainy days of the business, rather than its position on the long-range curve. Some "rainy days" can last a fairly long time. For investment banking there can be six or seven rather bad years of rain.

Another example of the difference between a short-term slump and the long-term decline of the curve is the business of a barber. Do you remember when the normal procedure for a man was to get a haircut every other week? Then, as longer hair became more fashionable, there could be an interval of many weeks between haircuts. As a matter of fact, a great many barbers were forced to quit because of the lack of work. When this change first took place I remember thinking that the business of cutting men's hair was on the downward slide to oblivion. I was dead wrong, of course.

The business of barbering was not heading toward its demise; it was only going through a painful but cyclical swing. The industry had a couple of good things going for it. First, hair keeps on growing. Also, the art of cutting hair was upgraded and began paying more, because long hair needed styling. Barbering has gone through an adverse cycle into one that transformed it into good business again.

Sometimes the normal life-span of a business can be cut short by sudden events or accidents, just like a person's life. An example would be if a business were to unexpectedly lose its location. A friend of mine had a doughnut shop that was quite successful on Crenshaw Boulevard in Los Angeles. The city created a divider on each side of the street that isolated my friend's store from the normal flow of traffic, and within a year the shop had to close.

Case histories will give you a better understanding of the

HITCH YOUR WAGON TO A STAR 71

life-span curve of a business. Let's look at some examples that are over the hill.

Business	Why Over the Hill
Manufacture of steam locomotives.	Obsolete due to better product.
Direct selling.	Waning due to cooling-off-period laws.
Watch repairing.	Obsolete due to electronic age.
Manufacture of large cars.	Obsolete due to high fuel cost.
Home-delivery bread trucks.	Obsolete due to supermarkets.

To sharpen your awareness, prepare a list of your own examples of businesses in the declining side of the curve.

It is much more rewarding to look at business possibilities on the growth side of the curve. To detect these possibilities start with needs that are expanding: these will be the source of ideas for businesses to satisfy those needs. They are the opportunities to seek out and hitch up to. Here are some expanding needs and businesses that relate to them. This list is intended to stimulate your research; not to make recommendations.

Expanding Need	Business
More leisure time.	Entertainment media; travel-oriented businesses such as tours, travel agencies, travel guides, sports-oriented businesses.
More working wives.	Convenience goods and services: house-cleaning services, day-care nurseries, convenience foods.

Expanding Need	Business
High energy costs.	Home insulation, more efficient transportation, solar water heating.
Labor savings.	Computers, labor-saving building materials. Inventions and innovations that save labor.
Health.	Quit-smoking clinic, exercise equipment, health foods, health club, private tennis club.

The most important step in planning your business is to couple what you like to do with a business that satisfies an expanding need. Most of us do not bother to go through this step, but it is the cheapest form of insurance for success.

Great results can come from simple combinations. I subscribe to a magazine called *Runner's World.* In a recent issue there was an editorial by the owner telling a little about his background. Bob Anderson is twenty-nine years old and has been running since he was fourteen. He still runs between twenty and twenty-five miles per week. While in high school he had a great desire to learn more about running, but found there was no published magazine on the subject. So, with an initial investment of $100, he decided to start his own magazine. That was twelve years ago.

Now *Runner's World* has a circulation of 275,000, and this entrepreneur has clearly been successful. He hitched his wagon (love of running) to a star (the large and expanding interest in running).

Let us assume for a moment that another person was interested in painting black vases rather than running. Visualize a fellow who, from his childhood, had an intense interest in painting black vases. Since he was unable to find a magazine

HITCH YOUR WAGON TO A STAR 73

on the subject, let's also assume he started his own magazine, "Black Vase Painter's World."

Where do you suppose this fellow would be today? Well, his magazine business would be in oblivion. While he had a great love for painting black vases, it just did not happen to be an expanding business opportunity. He did not have the good fortune or good sense of Bob Anderson, who had a keen interest in a field that was just at the right point of the curve.

Many businesses inherently have long life-spans, and do not have the risk of an irreversible downslide. Such stable businesses include hardware stores, food markets, and repair services. Sometimes a basically stable business seems to be in a decline, but in most cases it is not in a decline but only a cyclical change.

The old-fashioned mom-and-pop grocery store was a textbook example of a business that had been written off, replaced by the supermarkets. But now the old mom-and-pop store is enjoying a robust revival. The Southland Corporation of Texas, which owns the chain of 7-11 stores, now has over 7000 of these units in operation. It is the "rebirth" of a business that was never really dead at all: the small convenience market.

On the other hand, you may be in a business that is clearly on the downhill side of the curve. You must broaden your perspective so the business will incorporate activities that are not going in the same downward direction as your earlier operation.

Let's assume your business was building the best steam locomotives in the world. The locomotive is on a downward curve in sales, so if you were to persist in building them, you would end up on a devastating ride downhill. Your product has been made obsolete by technological advances, and there are other machines that will do the job better and at less cost.

Here is where you can change your business curve by changing your perspective, switching to a wide-angle lens. As a manufacturer of steam locomotives, you are clearly doomed, but what if you were to redefine your business as one of being simply in the field of transportation? Now you have broken out of your downward spiral. With this broader perspective you can apply your knowledge, assets, and people to fulfilling needs. If the need is filled by manufacturing diesel-powered locomotives, you change accordingly. You have transformed your downward sine curve into an upward one.

Here is an example of a company that did not respond by broadening its scope, and as a result lost out. When I worked for Johns-Manville, in the late 1950s, my specialty was industrial products that included insulation materials. In the field of cold-storage insulation, Johns-Manville had a product called Rock Cork that had been introduced in 1907. By the 1950s there were many advancements in cold-storage insulation, including dramatically new products that were put on the market by competitors: Fiberglas, Foamglass, Styrofoam, polyurethane, and others.

Unfortunately, Johns-Manville took the position that its business was Rock Cork, and Rock Cork went right down the tubes because it could not compete with new modern materials. Had J-M used the wide-angle-lens approach of being in business to sell cold-storage insulation rather than Rock Cork insulation, they would have maintained and expanded their market by utilizing whatever products served customers best.

You are going to operate only one business. Why not have everything going for you, including the life-cycle curve? Don't hitch your wagon to a dead horse. Hitch it to a *star!*

10
SPECIALIZE

As the world has become more complex and densely populated, specialization has emerged. Specialization increases as knowledge expands. Since population and knowledge will both continue to expand, it becomes clear that specialization will play a more important role in our lives.

Medicine provides us with an example of how specialization has evolved. It would not have made sense for the country doctor in a sparsely populated area to be a specialist, but with our present density of population and greater scope of medical knowledge, the general practitioner is a rarity.

Our society is so highly developed that a business must be more effective in order to survive. To become more effective, it must be more specialized. Consumers are accepting specialization as the best way to fill needs for products and services. When your children think of a hamburger, who do they think of? Probably McDonald's or some similar place.

One fact about specialization is of importance to anyone going into a new business: people who specialize seem to have more successful businesses than those who do not. There is a simple explanation for this. Specialists are better at what they do because they concentrate on a smaller target and so are better at it than nonspecialists. The specialist will attract business away from the nonspecialist, and the more business he attracts, the greater is his capability of getting still better, which results in even more business—and upward goes the spiral.

There is another reason to seriously consider specialization: it has fewer risks. For one, there will be fewer unknowns to contend with. Once your experience teaches you how to make your business work, you have invented your pattern of success. If you are inclined to expand, you can do so, without experiencing other unknown risks. Therefore, specialization will reduce the variables you must cope with, both before you start and after you begin operating. Running a business should not be like straightening out a bucket of worms. In business, surprises are usually problems, and specialization will reduce the number of surprises that pop out of the woodwork.

To stimulate your own thoughts on specialization, I have listed here some business categories. After each one, using Column 1, write in the name of the most successful company or individual you know of.

	Column 1	Column 2
CANDY		
ICE CREAM		
CHICKEN		
WASHING MACHINES		
MUFFLERS		
DOCTOR		
LAWYER		
REALTOR		
DOUGHNUT SHOP		
MECHANIC		
BUILDER		
SALESMAN		

In Column 2, rate each one as to how specialized it is. Use a scale of one to ten, with the highest score of ten going to an absolute specialist and a score of zero for a generalized business. Once you have completed Column 2, you can calculate the average degree of specialization of these firms. You will very likely see that there is a correlation between specialization and success.

You might expand this study to include companies in your own field to see if there is a similar correlation. If your survey shows that specialists do better in your own business, you will want to consider this in your planning.

The benefits of being specialized can be seen in case histories. R & B Development Company developed and still owns 7000 apartment units throughout the country. Until they hit upon their own specialty, they were a small developer. They then created a concept in apartment living that offered a specialized environment for one kind of tenant: the young, single person. The first R & B project built under this concept charged rents that were well above prices for comparable apartments. They immediately had 100 percent occupancy at these high rents, and this specialty became their ticket to success. They had created the swinging-single apartment complex.

Here is another fellow who found the Midas touch to success through specialization. When you think of "muffler," you probably think of Midas. At the time the Midas muffler concept was created, the idea of having a store that sold nothing but mufflers sounded crazy. On the other hand, how could anyone do a better job on your muffler problem than a man whose livelihood depended on it? This specialized business also filled a need widespread enough to make it work. It certainly would not have worked in 1920, but as our world becomes more populated (in this case with cars), spectacular opportunities arise through specialization.

Therefore, specialization must be timely. As Solomon declares, there is a time for everything. You must be able to couple specialization with a density of demand that makes it work. There are some businesses in which specialization seems to be carried to an extreme. Cookie shops are successful, but only in locations of very high walking traffic that provide great impulse purchasing power.

Alfred Hitchcock was a successful motion picture producer who enhanced his career by gaining a reputation as a specialist. His specialty, of course, was suspense. By devoting his career to this one field, he put all of his cumulative experience into each new production. This produced work that set him apart.

Real estate is a business for specialists. Be a shopping center developer, or an industrial developer, or a specialized broker, or an office building specialist, or apartment specialist, but don't try to do it all. There is just too much to learn and experience in each field. If you try to do it all, you will be outclassed . . . by specialists.

We can learn compelling lessons on specialization from food operations. Brookdale Ice Cream Company is no longer in business, but for a number of years they grew into a chain of fine ice cream stores. As you might imagine, ice cream sells better in summer than in winter. So the owners came up with a perfectly logical idea: why not add some other food product that sells better in the winter? Their choice of the second food line was doughnuts because these sell best when it is cold. Great idea, right? Wrong. Instead of doubling their sales, the sales stayed at the same level as when they sold only ice cream.

Now, however, they had two entirely different operations going in each store: different equipment, different know-how, different everything. They could not do as good a job as when all of their attention was on one product line. Also, they lost their identity as an ice cream store. Their image became blurred. Their customers no longer had a clear picture of "Brookdale" meaning "ice cream" anymore. Ultimately this fine company went out of business.

In some food lines, you simply must consider specialization. To gain recognition as the best there is, you must satisfy your customer's specialized appetite. The kiss of death for a doughnut shop is to start selling ice cream, or hot dogs, or hamburgers, or anything other than doughnuts. With the addition of any other product, a doughnut shop is simply no longer a doughnut shop; it becomes just another hot dog stand.

Associated Hosts is a large, publicly held company that is successful in operating numerous restaurant concepts under a number of names: Smuggler's Inn, Bombay Bicycle Club, Julie's Place, Ponderosa, and others. They have all reflected the creativity of the founder, Joe Bulasky. Opening new restaurants with different themes is surely a creative challenge, but some benefits of specialization are lost. One of their early restaurants was a fine coffee shop called Coffee Dan's, and in my opinion their success would have been even greater had all of their efforts gone into the proliferation of that one concept.

While Associated Hosts did not specialize, they have nevertheless built a successful company. However, you must keep in mind that the entrepreneur who must continually create new concepts rather than specialize in one has two problems. He misses the greatest opportunity for growth, and he may be courting disaster. New undertakings are inherently risky because you are treading on unfamiliar ground. Those who specialize are on familiar ground and therefore have a much greater incidence of success. Had Associated Hosts gone into new concepts that flopped, their earlier successes could have been nullified.

Food, therefore, is surely an appropriate field for specialization. Can you imagine a restaurant being in existence for forty years, with a throng waiting for dinner every night, and having only one item on the menu? Lawry's Prime Rib Restaurant on La Cienega Boulevard in Los Angeles is a gold-medal example of successful specialization. How could anybody not do one thing well?

One California company has expressed its views about specialization by changes in its name. The company started and grew under the name "Abbey Rents." Then some years ago, Abbey Rents changed their name to "Abbey Rents and Sells." In addition to their specialty of renting equipment, they began to sell. Recently they have changed their name back again to Abbey Rents. It is an interesting story of success based on a specialty, which then broadened into other areas and finally got back into the specialized business from which it began.

Many specialized businesses are outgrowths of their owners' previous experience. Recently I visited a prosperous gift shop in a small town in northern California. The owner had been an equipment salesman to butcher shops, selling knives, wooden chopping blocks, and various utensils used by butchers and cooks. The merchandise in his store reflects this background and adheres rather steadfastly to the line he knew best. The result is an assortment of utensils that are both unusual and interesting. He stuck to his specialty.

A recent success story was created by someone whose specialty never existed before. As it happened, the specialty filled a widespread need and is now growing rapidly. The business is called "Tune-Up Masters." It was started by a mechanic who specialized in tune-up work, and who felt that the public was being cheated. So he created a new company that tunes up cars for a fixed fee: that is all they do. They have never charged more than the advertised price. If a company does nothing but tune up cars, it seems to me they are going to know something about what they're doing.

My friend Frank Milne, who is owner of a Chevrolet agency, has been number one in Corvette sales in the United States for years. When the Corvettes first came out, he decided that the agency would specialize in them. They started off with a big investment in inventories of cars and parts. They sponsored races. They gave special incentives to salesmen. Mechanics and body men were trained for specialized Corvette work. This specialization resulted in a leadership momentum that has lasted for twenty-five years.

In contrast, I have another friend who was a pioneer in selling imported cars. As the imports caught on, he became quite successful, but he was always unwilling to specialize as a dealer for any one particular make. He had the pick of the crop, due to his experience dating back to the first days of imported car sales. He decided it was better to have a dealership where numerous makes were sold under one roof, but by not specializing, he missed getting into the big leagues. Volkswagen, Datsun, and all the others who demanded specialization finally passed him by.

As entrepreneurs, we should enjoy the benefits of specialization if for no other reason than that it will enhance our chance for success. You probably have heard the three secrets to success in real estate: location, location, location. Well, perhaps the way to success in your own business is to follow the three secrets of business: specialize, specialize, and specialize.

For the business you are considering, make up a list of possible areas of specialization. Then look around and see if they have been proved out in operating businesses. Follow the proven winners, unless you are a real pioneer such as the man from Tune-Up Masters who created a successful specialty by meeting a new and enlarging need.

There is no question in my mind that your chances for success will be enhanced by operating as a specialist. Some successful specialists will stick to their specialties through long careers. Others, however, will use the power of specialization to get into a new business, and then from this platform, branch out into other areas of endeavor. For them, specialization is an ace card for getting started.

Keep in mind, too, that specialists who are winners must be prudent in how they broaden out from their specialty. The rocks and shoals of business are strewn with winners in one specialized field who went down in other, unfamiliar seas.

11
NOW: DECIDE WHAT BUSINESS

You are now completing Step Two: "What and Where?" These chapters have provided you with the elements to be considered for your decision. There are just a few—but very important—ingredients:

Do what you like to do.
Fill a need.
Hitch your wagon to a star.
Specialize.

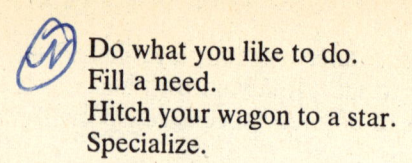

Perhaps the most important decision you will make is what business to start. Some years ago I came across a neat definition of the art of business in *Fortune* magazine: "The art of business is the art of making irrevocable decisions based upon incomplete information." Decisions will be better as we become better informed.

To decide on a business is to make essentially an irrevocable decision. Your chances for success will improve if you gather the maximum amount of information you can to support your decision. Therefore the chapter headings above should all be included in your overall evaluation that results in a decision.

An airline pilot uses a checklist before he takes off to be sure that nothing is overlooked. So let's use our own checklist to go a step further. In addition to checking off each item (in our case it is a chapter heading), let's assign values to each. On a scale of one to ten, we will assign a score. A score of ten means the maximum degree of conformity. A score of zero means we have not met the criteria for that item.

Here is an example of how a checklist can be used by anyone deciding on a business. The entrepreneur is named Joe. During high school, he worked part time for an auto-towing service. On graduating, Joe began working full time for the towing service. He has worked for them for two years. Obviously, he knows something about towing. Joe is also good at buying used cars, fixing them up, and reselling them at a profit. He also has a flair as an auto mechanic.

With this background, Joe wants to consider three possible businesses:

1. Start a tow service.
2. Operate a used car lot.
3. Start an auto repair business.

Here is a checklist that Joe might have filled out:

WHAT AND WHERE CHECKLIST

SCORE: 0 to 10

Item	Towing Service	Used Car Lot	Auto Repair Service
Do what you like to do.	6	0	10
Fill a need.	10	5	10
Hitch your wagon to a star.	8	6	9
Specialize.	10	?	10

In reviewing the checklist, we can draw a number of conclusions. The used car lot doesn't seem to be a very good idea. The towing service and the auto repair business are worthy of consideration. Based purely on the numerical totals, the auto repair business wins out. Let's assume that Joe's decision is to look carefully at starting an auto repair business. Then the previous four chapters should be reviewed again and in much more detail, with only that business in mind.

Don't let the total scoring of your analysis mislead you. Let's assume an airline pilot has ten items to check before taking off. He finds that every item is perfect except one, the condition of his tires, which are dangerously worn. His flight is in danger because of one serious deficiency. For you, each of the four checklist items must score well to insure success.

In deciding which business to start, you'll find that the checklist becomes a framework for objective analysis. This systematic approach should become natural too. To achieve it, practice using the checklist, because learning is a process of repetition. As with driving a car with a clutch, after repeated use and practice you begin operating the clutch and gear changes automatically.

You can make up your own analysis form. In fact, make a couple of dozen copies and use them to score people you know who operate their own business. It will be interesting to see the correlation between a person having a high score and one who is successful.

List businesses you might like to look into, and run each one through your checklist. You will become more familiar with each possibility on the list, and you will gain increased familiarity with each of the "What and Where?" chapters. You will also gain confidence in dealing with their implications when looking at any potential business.

You may already have a business in mind that you plan to start. No matter how appealing the prospects seem, do not overlook your checklist appraisal. It may indeed verify and reinforce your choice. On the other hand, the clear light of objective scrutiny may create serious doubts. The checklist may uncover fatal defects. Before making your final selection, a number of businesses may be ruled out. Keep seeking the one that makes sense under your checklist appraisal.

The entire process of "what and where?" appraisals could take place over a considerable period of time. I have two suggestions for you. First, don't burn your bridges. Presumably you are working for someone else while you are considering a business of your own. By continuing to work, you earn a living and probably save money for seed capital. Also, you are not under pressure to act. If you're not working, you must ultimately act or go back to work. The longer you are out of work, the greater the chance of making an error in judgment through impatience. You will have much better equilibrium by continuing to work.

Also, I suggest you be exceedingly patient in seeking out and deciding on your business. The natural tendency is to act too early rather than too late. For some, the process will take a long time and this is fine. For others it can come early. The time it takes has nothing to do with anyone else; it is unique to your own circumstances.

This chapter summarizes what you need to answer the second-step question on starting a business, "What and Where?" Once this second step is answered, you can proceed into the preparation phase, "Planning the Attack."

STEP THREE

PLANNING THE ATTACK

Before you start, you had better be ready. If you are not prepared, you are going to get slaughtered. This step will provide you with a checklist of ammunition to have stockpiled.

12
PARTNERS

At this stage you have decided to become an entrepreneur, and have determined what business to be in and where to locate. Now some planning must take place before any business activities or obligations are undertaken.

The subjects covered in Step Three, "Planning the Attack," will prepare you. The first consideration is whether you should be on your own or start with a partner.

Think back for a minute to high school chemistry. Litmus paper was the small strip of paper you dipped into a liquid to determine if it was acid or alkaline. If the paper turned red, the solution was acid; and if it turned blue, the solution was alkaline.

During our lifetimes, we all have experiences in some form of partnerships. Some can be gloriously rewarding and others can be just deadly. Wouldn't it be wonderful if, before entering into a partnership, we could reduce it to a solution and use a litmus paper test to forewarn us whether the partnership would be a success or failure?

How do you test a potential partnership before jumping into it? The first purpose of this chapter is to provide you with a simple testing procedure to evaluate a partnership before making your decision. The second purpose is to provide you with some hints on making your partnership a good one. So there is a dual goal here. First to judge before going in; and then once in, to make it work.

You should know how to test a partnership, even though you presently have no plans whatsoever to get involved in one. Business partnerships can unexpectedly arise out of circumstances or opportunities that may very well merit consideration.

Partnerships can be hard to evaluate because they are in subjective territory and can be influenced by emotional considerations. Our procedure will evaluate a potential partnership based on its inherent strengths or weaknesses, and eliminate subjective considerations.

Let's first clear up what I mean by business partners. I am referring to a corporation that is run with more than one managing owner. The usual case would be two individuals who co-own the corporation and who both work full time at it.

There is a legal form of business called a "partnership." Partnerships, as covered in this chapter, have nothing to do with the legal "partnership" relationship. The legal entity you should use is a corporation. This would be true whether you were operating by yourself or with another person.

The problem with a legal partnership is one of liability. Each partner becomes personally responsible for the partnership liabilities of the other. A corporation is a perpetual entity which can be made up of one or more persons. If you are by yourself, you're going to be president. If you have a partner, you must decide on your respective titles and roles.

Many singularly successful men could never operate with partners. A very strong individual with great drive, intellect, ego, and capacity for extraordinary hard work would not be a very likely candidate for a partner. Such a person wouldn't need one. Also, the dilution of authority and ownership that is inherent in a partnership might not be acceptable to a power-house entrepreneur. For example, I just cannot imagine someone like Howard Hughes or J. Paul Getty operating with corporate partners.

However, men like Hughes or Getty are rare. That leaves a vast majority of entrepreneurs who could very well opt for partnership. Incredible success stories have emerged from partnerships, including the largest merchandising operation in the world, Sears Roebuck. If you put your mind to it, you will discover that partnerships have worked in virtually all fields of business. Some had been family partnerships, such as Lever Brothers and Brooks Brothers. Others, such as Baskin-Robbins ice cream, have become the largest in their fields. On and on. So, while everyone has some favorite horror story concerning partnerships, the teaming together of businessmen has resulted in mighty success stories.

When and if you face the decision of partnership versus go-it-alone, you will be at an absolutely critical crossroad. A good partnership in business can be enormously effective and rewarding. I know because I am fortunate enough to be in that position. A poor business partnership, even with honest and well-meaning partners, can be the ultimate form of frustration. I have experienced that too. I will show you how to pick a winner and also how to expose what might be a loser.

A good partnership requires the presence of two paradoxical elements. First, you must be very much alike. Second, in another way, you must be clearly unlike your prospective partner. The trick is that both elements be present, in the right order.

First, let's identify the area in which you should be alike. You should have similar backgrounds. In many ways, a business partnership has much in common with a marriage. Certain guidelines used in judging the success or failure in a marriage can be applied to judging the prospects of a partnership.

Marriages between people who have nothing in common can be doomed before they start. The greatest chance of success in a marriage exists for a couple who have similar backgrounds. One reason is that they can communicate easily. They know what is on each other's mind, and how to be supportive of each other. Their goals and life-styles will be similar, too. These common traits, shared, form a strong bond that holds them together through thick and thin.

So it is with business partners. Similar backgrounds will provide the commonality to stay in harness together, through good times and bad. In good times partners must share a sense of prudence and in bad times they must share an attitude of steadfastness. Being alike in background will keep them more easily in tune with one another.

In other ways, business partners should not be alike. They should complement each other in their business expertise and experiences. One difficulty a single business person can encounter is that his experience may not be sufficiently broad in all aspects of his business. For example, a person might be expert in marketing widgets but be completely inexperienced when it comes to manufacturing them. It might therefore make sense for him to team up with a partner who has production expertise. It certainly would make no sense at all for him to become partners with someone whose expertise was the same as his own.

So our litmus paper test for potential partners must identify two essential ingredients. First, are the people of similar backgrounds, with similar goals and ethics, which will produce mutual supportiveness and complete communication? Second, are their areas of expertise complementary to each other so the overall structure will have greater strength than that represented by each individually?

In addition to evaluating the two essential ingredients for a partnership, you should also weigh the pros and cons of it. As with any critical decision in our lives, it is usually helpful to sit down and write the "for" and "against" of a question. This forces us to think, and sometimes the answers become readily apparent. Make up a list as part of your evaluation of having a prospective partner. Here is a sample:

I have hiked the entrepreneurial trail both ways: as a sole owner and with partners. My partnerships have been both good and bad. I'll outline these experiences and show what made one partnership work and why another did not work. Also, I'll include other partnership case studies that will illustrate some do's and don'ts.

For	Against
1. Safety: it takes two to decide; reduces chances of going off half-cocked.	**1.** Dilution of ownership rewards.
2. Avoid unremitting and lonely responsibility of being sole owner. Take time for vacations, etc.	**2.** Loss of complete authority.
3. Have a highly motivated coworker (by virtue of co-ownership).	**3.** Sharing of recognition.
4. Have knowledge and experience complementary to mine.	**4.** A partner's poor judgment would hurt me and company.
5. Have someone to share problems with.	**5.** Risk of a falling-out.

My first business experience as an entrepreneur was with a partner. I had resigned from Johns-Manville and purchased an option to buy one-half the stock in National Donut Corporation. National Donut was a one-man, small, undercapitalized company in Los Angeles that made automatic doughnut-production machines. The founder, Virgil Ackles, was a great machine designer and a superb salesman. Unfortunately we really didn't have much in common.

Virgil and I were unsuccessful as partners because of our utter dissimilarities. He was twenty years older than I, and we were absolutely different in our approach to things. We didn't have common goals or language. Virgil had been a dyed-in-the-wool one-man band for many years. He had taken me in as a partner because he needed money badly, and was without any working capital.

I had gone in to turn the company around. My attorney advised me that my investment should be made as a loan, and I should have the loan convertible into 50 percent of the company's stock at a later date. If I had initially purchased stock and the company failed, then as an officer and stockholder I could have become personally responsible for liabilities such as federal and state withholding taxes that flow through to the officers. This is a good example of the value of consulting an attorney whenever you enter business.

Virgil and I were simply different breeds. For example, while he was an incurable innovator, I wanted to freeze the designs of our machines. We bogged down because we failed the first requirement; we did not have similar backgrounds. After eighteen traumatic months, we sold the company to Pillsbury, and luckily we both escaped with our family jewels intact. It was not a good partnership; it was like a marriage between two people who did not speak the same language.

After the sale of National Donut, I began Holland Construction Company. Over a period of ten years I operated the business as sole owner. I would have to summarize this period as being one during which I became eccentric; that is to say, unbalanced. I spent more time on business and less on family and leisure than I should have. I felt I had to be an example of the work ethic to my employees. I was first in the office in the morning, and usually last to leave. On the affirmative side, I must say that the challenge and the recognition were nice: it was all mine.

I started the business I am now in, Yum Yum Donut Shops, as the sole owner. Two and a half years later I had three shops operating profitably and the foundation was laid for a chain of shops. I had run an advertisement in the *Los Angeles Times* classified section for a real estate manager, to work on new shop locations. Out of sixty replies to my little ad there was one that shone out like a beacon: a letter and résumé sent by Frank Watase.

Here was a man of my age who had a terrific background in multiple-store management experience, and an MBA degree from Harvard Business School. Well, Frank and I set up a date to meet and talk. We talked for days.

In our conversations, Frank expressed an interest in having more than an employee or agent relationship. In the past he had worked for others, and he was at a point in his life where he was interested in becoming an entrepreneur. I gave this a great deal of thought. My prior experience with a partner had not been good; and my prior experience on my own had resulted in an unbalanced life.

My decision was not clouded by money. There are times when a business owner takes in a partner because he needs money (as was the case with Virgil Ackles), or he receives a lot of money to give up part ownership. What I had in Yum Yum was two and a half years of sweat equity. On the balance sheet, the book value of the company was still only $500. Frank, at the same time, didn't have any money to put up. His savings had been tied up in a Hawaiian construction venture that might take years to pay off. So, from the standpoint of money, my decision would be a pure one; it would not be clouded by receiving any money from selling part of the business to a partner. It would be like a marriage without a dowry.

The situation from which my decision would have to be made was this:

1. I had a going and growing business (three shops);
2. I owned it 100 percent.

Should I proceed as a 100 percent owner or take in a partner; if a partner, on what basis? I decided to take in a partner, with Frank having an immediate, no-strings-attached ownership of 50 percent of the company. I sold Frank the stock for its book value: $250. My reasons for bringing in Frank as an equal partner were as follows.

First, I felt a strong rapport with him about the company's future. We both wanted a big company. Also, our business backgrounds complemented each other's. Frank's background was in multiple-store operations and merchandising, even though he responded to an ad for a real estate expert. My background was in real estate development, even though my efforts for two and a half years were in learning the doughnut business. Also, we were personally responsive to each other. There was a sense of mutual regard. Frank and I had similar backgrounds with respect to age, education, personal attitudes, business experiences and hardships, and work habits.

Finally, I wanted someone to share the load. The unremitting responsibility of being alone can wear thin. I had observed the example of two men, my friend Bob Silvers and his partner Ben Garfinkle, who were in business together with fine results. They divided responsibilities according to their capabilities. Ben was the driving force in sales, and Bob was the inside man, controlling finances and operations. Each of them took long vacations every year. (I remembered this with a sense of envy during the years I was on my own.) Together, they built a large and profitable operation. I had Bob's and Ben's example to help me recognize the benefits that a good partnership can offer.

Shortly before I met Frank, another event had occurred in my life that gave me a different perspective on business. Jamie, my fifteen-year-old son, had contracted leukemia. My business up to that time had been the dominant activity in my life. I began to realize what a foolish eccentricity this can become.

Thus, Frank Watase became my partner. My friends thought I had gone bananas. It was the smartest business decision I have ever made in my life. Like getting married, it was the luck of finding the right mate. Our partnership works.

What makes it work? It can all be boiled down to the fundamentals: we were alike in background and were complementary in our business capabilities. The result was an incredibly supportive and communicative relationship. Also, you must understand that our partnership works because we work at making it work. It is not a perpetual motion machine.

During the first year or so there were adjustments, learning, a certain amount of disagreement, and lots of communicating that went on before we began to work as a smooth team. On my part, I was no longer the sole proprietor, making decisions entirely on my own. This adjustment came fairly easily, because I felt good having a partner contribute to decision making.

On Frank's part, the greatest adjustment was in learning

the doughnut business, and focusing on our specialized operation. So our first year was one of adjusting to the partnership and getting ourselves into gear so that each was performing in his most effective area, and at the same time supporting the other in his role, too.

As the partnership matured, it became more effective. More and more, we appreciate the other's contributions and skills. When there are differences on issues, we let our views hang out, and as stubborn and articulate as we both can be, we talk out areas of differences until we have agreement.

I have referred to the successful partnership of Bob Silvers and Ben Garfinkle which influenced my decision to join up with Frank Watase. Their partnership has the crucial elements for success. While their personalities differed, their backgrounds had a great deal in common. With respect to business talents, Bob and Ben are not the same at all. Together, they formed a team that absolutely baffled their cynical critics who felt their business venture together would end in early disaster.

Starting a business with a partner is a critical time to have a first-class corporation lawyer. Be very selective in deciding on your lawyer. Find and pay for the very best.

Being in business with a partner will require a buy-sell agreement to provide for an orderly continuation of the business in the event of the death of one of the partners. Life insurance proceeds allow the corporation to purchase the stock of the deceased partner. Again, this is a system that your lawyer will set up.

There are specific guidelines in deciding whether you should have a partner.

1. Does your situation call for a partner?
2. Does your prospective partnership meet these tests:
    a. Are you similar in personal backgrounds and goals?
    b. Are you complementary in what you can contribute to the corporation as to business expertise?

>   **3.** Does your own "for" and "against" list lead you to a decision?
>
>   **4.** Are you both the type of person who can work in harness with a co-owner?

Together, these checkoff items will give you an objective platform from which to make your decision. If you decide on a partnership venture, you must then make it work. The success of your business now hinges on the success of your partnership. Like making a garden bear fruit, you will want to use every tool available to insure the harvest.

First, develop total communication with each other. Communicate daily on any item of business for which one wants the support or advice of the other. Eliminate surprises by getting agreement on significant issues before acting on them.

Communication clears up differences. When problems are brought out into the open, the very act of communication causes them to be resolved and therefore to disappear. It is important that each and every major operating policy of the company be thrashed out until there is agreement. There should not be one single significant policy in force that does not have the support of both partners. If there is disagreement, it must be cleared up before subordinate management is brought into the picture. In this way, staff managers who receive policy decisions know that they are getting company policy, and not the policy of one partner which might be subject to the objection of the other partner. It avoids any possibility of employees finding themselves in the cross fire of different instructions from partners.

Another tool that will help your partnership is veto power. If an issue arises in which the partners are absolutely settled on opposite views, then there should be a clear understanding that one partner's veto in the matter will be respected by the other partner. This means that none of your operating policies will be put into effect unless both partners are in accord. If this were not so, there would be a terrible risk of management breakdown.

Another important tool in keeping the partnership garden healthy and fruitful is that both partners must be very careful not to criticize. A business is managed by exceptions, which means that a manager should be concerned with the exceptions, or problems. Heaven knows, business is not business without problems. But there is a fine art to discussing a problem without expressing it in the form of a criticism.

The thing to remember is: never, never criticize. Discuss, explore, suggest, recommend, implore, pull, but never criticize.

Since there is merit in listening to the advice of wise men, let's go back to Solomon again. He had something to say in favor of partnerships: "Two can accomplish more than twice as much as one, for the results can be much better. If one falls, the other pulls him up; but if a man falls when he is alone, he's in trouble. . . . And one standing alone can be attacked and defeated, but two can stand back to back and conquer; three is even better, for a triple-braided cord is not easily broken."

There is, finally, one ultimate secret of success in making a partnership work. It is to follow the definition of the word "love," as expressed by Paul of Tarsus. Paul shows how to insure success. If you can apply his definition of love to your relationship with your partner, you will have found the key to a successful partnership. Type it out on a small piece of paper and read it every day:

> Love is very patient and kind, never jealous or envious, never boastful or proud, never haughty or selfish or rude. Love does not demand its own way. It is not irritable or touchy. It does not hold grudges and will hardly even notice when others do it wrong. It is never glad about injustice, but rejoices whenever truth wins out. If you love someone you will be loyal to him no matter what the cost. You will always believe in him, always expect the best of him, and always stand your ground in defending him.

13
LEARN BY DOING

Pretend for a minute that this is a book for tennis. Your purpose in reading it is to learn how to become a tennis player. By any stretch of your imagination, can you see the possibility of accomplishing that goal without spending time on a tennis court? What if I told you that you could become a great tennis player without actually playing the game at all? You would think I was silly. If you were ever to be a competent tennis player, you must first practice long and hard at it.

Then why is it that so many go into a business without ever practicing on the court it's played on? I am experienced in this subject. Not only did I enter into a game in which I had never been on the court, but I bet all of my family jewels that I would win. This is like playing Russian roulette with all the chambers loaded. Naturally, I lost the game and my savings.

It is easy for you to understand the tennis analogy, but I want you to know that a great number of sincere people cannot apply this simple principle when it comes to playing the game of business. Simply stated, the principle (let's call it the "learn by doing" doctrine) is: you cannot succeed in a business unless you personally have had prior training and practice in that business.

Now, if you have never had experience in the business you plan to start, what do you do? You simply experience it before you start. If you are going to open a doughnut shop, you must learn by working at it. What you learn must be complete. You must become a competent baker, keep the store clean, mop floors, wash windows, take out the trash. You must learn to do bookkeeping, purchasing, merchandising, and every other function that makes a doughnut shop tick.

To learn a business before starting up is really easy to do. You just work for someone who is already in the business. In fact, you should work for as many people and in enough capacities that you become an expert in the whole business. Then you have bought your ticket for success in that field. Since you have already learned the business by experiencing it, when you start your own you should have every reason to do well in it.

Let me give you two examples of "learn by doing." First, the wrong approach. Here I speak as an authority, because it happened to me. I had a successful construction business and during a slack period, I had the idea of starting a chain of franchised Mexican restaurants. My firm had fine capabilities in architecture, construction, and real estate development, but no experience in the restaurant industry or in Mexican food. I thought that since the restaurant field was so full of competent managers, I would delegate this area of responsibility to people whom I would recruit. Can you picture a tennis match with a player "delegating" his serve, or lob, or forehand? The results in my case were so disastrous that I am going to stress again the "learn by doing" doctrine. You cannot succeed in a business unless you personally have had prior training and practice in that business.

Now for example number two. This is a story about someone else who decided to go into the restaurant business. His experience had been in an entirely different field, not a particularly good training ground. He had been an actor. Before starting his restaurant he decided to specialize in only one dish and it would be something he particularly liked: chili. While he was very fond of chili, he had no experience in making it. At this point he reached a crucial decision. As he didn't have money, he decided to hole up in the home of friends and devote all of his time to experimenting and developing the best chili he could create. He spent six months doing nothing else, and after this period he was satisfied that he had developed a recipe for the very best chili possible.

Next, he opened his restaurant. This unemployed actor had prepared himself by spending six months "learning by doing." His name was Dave Chasen, and Chasen's in Beverly Hills became one of the great restaurants in the world. Dave Chasen learned by doing *before* he opened.

Many issues of *Fortune* magazine contain articles about "professional managers." A professional manager is a special breed who can turn around large, sick businesses. They are found in conglomerates, sometimes global in operations. One characteristic of a professional manager is that he probably has not learned by doing. He has not had operating experience in the business he manages. These people are probably the brightest managers in the world. They are the superelite.

Their world is totally different from yours. Don't make the mistake of classifying yourself as a professional manager, which would make you exempt from the need of learning by doing. If you were a professional manager, you would probably not be considering your own business at all; you would be chased by banks who are seeking solutions for their ailing clients. For us ordinary folks, it's "learn by doing."

14

QUALITY WITHOUT COMPROMISE

When we go into business, we very earnestly want to be successful. I suppose if we could buy a pill that would insure success, we would spend all of our savings to have it. As a matter of fact, it is entirely possible that success in business can depend on one single pill, which if swallowed will result in success. The pill I am going to suggest is one you will have to formulate yourself, depending on the nature of your business.

But I am going to tell you its one active ingredient: quality without compromise. In this chapter I will refer to it as "QWC."

Business empires are built on this single ingredient, and I will describe some of them for you. But if you think this is an easy pill to swallow, you are in for a big surprise. The successful application of QWC is difficult and rarely achieved. If you can accomplish it, it could be your ticket to success.

Let's try to understand why the application of quality without compromise is so difficult. We will all stand up and loudly proclaim, as we march into the battleground of business, that we absolutely and unequivocally intend to sell the best: quality without compromise. What fools us is that in order to sell the best, we must buy the best. And here is where the casualties take place, because it is very difficult to buy the best.

For example, when was the last time you went into a shoe store and told the salesperson you wanted to buy the most expensive pair of shoes in the store? Or when did you last ask your butcher to cut you the most expensive steak in the market? Or when did you last pick out the most expensive vodka at the liquor store?

You see, when buying, we normally follow the irresistible urge to do the very opposite of what our key ingredient QWC requires us to do. When buying, we look for the best price and not for the best product. If you haven't been buying the most expensive vodka, can you imagine how difficult this practice is in business, when you are purchasing in the price-cutting, corner-cutting, discount battlefield of competition?

To swallow the magic pill QWC, you must buy the best of whatever raw materials make up your finished product, without compromise. The best is the most expensive. So therefore your purchasing policy must be to pay the highest price rather than the lowest price. This, as you can imagine, is hard for most of us to do.

By now you are getting the idea that QWC is a simple truth which in practice becomes hard to apply. Let's look at some examples.

I decided to apply the principle of QWC before opening the first Yum Yum Donut Shop. After the location of the store had been decided, I began lining up suppliers. Coffee is one of the most important products in a doughnut shop, and in Los Angeles there are a number of coffee suppliers who are good. I picked the one that had the best reputation for quality. This company sold a number of different grades of coffee. Now, to apply the principle of QWC, I ordered the top of the line, Mocha Java, which was sold to the most prestigious restaurants in town.

The first Yum Yum Shop was located in a low-income part of Los Angeles. Some people thought I was crazy to put Mocha Java in that doughnut shop. The general comment was that there was no way those customers would be able to tell the difference between Mocha Java and a more competitive brand. Well, you know, I really never found out whether the customers ever did know the difference. All I can tell you is the store is still selling 3000 cups of coffee per week, and we're still using Mocha Java. Why are we selling that much coffee? Who knows? With my tongue in cheek, I think the principle of quality without compromise had something to do with it.

I must confess that the expression "quality without compromise" belongs to someone else. In fact, there is a registered U.S. trademark that protects the phrase. It belongs to See's Candies of Los Angeles. They started in 1921 when Mrs. See began making candy in her kitchen, using the finest ingredients. They are a large company now, and there is still only one name for really fine candy in California and that is "See's." On every box of See's candy is their slogan: Quality Without Compromise.

Tom McGannis made a fortune operating one hamburger stand in Long Beach, California. I met Tom because he was the owner of a piece of commercial real estate that I was interested in leasing for a Yum Yum Donut Shop. For some months, I would go down to Tom's Long Beach hamburger stand and try to negotiate this real estate deal with him. I saw

QUALITY WITHOUT COMPROMISE 103

him quite a number of times and became utterly fascinated by his discourses on how the food business should be run, and by his success at operating his gold mine of a hamburger stand.

Tom had only one secret. Yes, you guessed it: QWC. In Southern California, there are a great number of Greeks who are in the hamburger business, including Tom. There were two other Greek operators who observed Tom's great success, and both of them thought they could share some of it. Both opened around the corner from Tom's so now there were three Greek hamburger stands within a stone's throw of each other.

The other two didn't even make a dent in Tom's business. And, according to Tom, they never even learned why. Tom was zapping them with his secret weapon: QWC. How did he do it? Well, for example, Tom believed that to make the best cheeseburger you must use 100 percent Cheddar Cheese. Not processed cheese or American or others; just 100 percent Cheddar. He would buy it in blocks and cut it up himself because real Cheddar could not be presliced.

His pickles were Heinz. His meat was graded to within 1 percent of fat content. Tom would personally go down to the wholesale produce market every morning at four o'clock to buy tomatoes; he would not depend on a produce distributor to pick out the best for him. Tom has his own recipe for chili, which he guarded the way Coca-Cola guards its formula. In every single ingredient, Tom was absolutely fanatical in buying the best. His sales volume was unreal, and to this day I am sure the other two Greeks never knew what hit them.

During those sessions in Tom McGannis's office, one example of QWC he cited was Colonel Sanders' chicken. Tom attributed its success to the fact that Colonel Sanders always bought chickens that were too good (that is, too expensive) to be sold in the markets. The public simply would not pay the price in the meat market for the quality raw product the colonel insisted on. While the public was unwilling to pay the price for this kind of chicken in the store, Colonel Sanders was smart enough to do so, and we all know the results.

The greatest success story in American fast-food history is surely McDonald's. Did you know that McDonald's was built on QWC? For example, at one time, McDonald units had basements. The basement was used to store sacks of Idaho potatoes, which were used to make French fries. The potatoes had to be peeled and cut up at each store before frying. Years of research were conducted before they decided to ship their French fries in the prepared state. The specifications for the frozen product, the equipment, and the shortening were so exacting that today the result is acknowledged as the world's best French fries.

McDonald's offers a very special lesson regarding the application of QWC. Selling price does not necessarily have to be higher because of purchasing the most expensive ingredients. Your selling price can actually be less than competitors with inferior ingredients, and for two reasons. First, the selling price can be controlled by exacting standards of portion control. In other words, if it is better, it doesn't have to be bigger. Also (and this is the real key), QWC inherently will add to your volume.

Remember when McDonald's first hit the public back in the 1950s? Their hamburger sold for, I believe, fifteen cents, and the big attraction was not quality but price. They did an enormous volume because of the great value, and still they applied QWC. It was the combination of widespread appeal (the hamburger) plus great value (a fifteen-cent price) plus QWC that put McDonald's into orbit. If you agree, then see if you can apply it in your own business.

If you stop and think about it, there are a number of success stories that have resulted from the magic pill QWC. One name that is very likely to come to mind is Sara Lee. Whenever you want a treat you will reach for Sara Lee, in the form of frozen sweet rolls, cakes, and other bakery products. The secret they apply is no secret at all because they have been boasting about it for years. They have never used a cheap type of shortening in their bakery products; they use only pure butter. Who else in the industry would be crazy enough to use nothing but butter? On the other hand, who else has achieved the fantastic success of Sara Lee?

QWC can become the cornerstone for word-of-mouth advertising. When the first Velvet Turtle restaurant opened in Redondo Beach, they had a policy of serving the most expensive brands of liquor in all of their mixed drinks. If you ordered a Scotch and soda, they poured Chivas Regal. If you ordered a martini, they poured Beefeater gin. The word got around fast that the Velvet Turtle served the most expensive brands of liquor rather than the customary "well" brands. This policy was evident every time they poured a drink, and it reinforced in the customers' minds that in all other respects the Velvet Turtle had quality without compromise.

The founder of the Velvet Turtle chain is a fellow named Wally Botello. One evening during the early days of the chain's success, his friends were gathered and the conversation drifted to the subject of the restaurant's enormous public acceptance. It was the consensus of his friends that success had resulted because of the ingeniously clever name Velvet Turtle. Wally Botello smiled and said that he could put up a sign that said "Sam's Cafe" and still be just as successful.

To prove his point, that is exactly what he did. One of his new restaurants was called, simply, Sam's Cafe. It, too, was every bit as successful as the others. Wally Botello knew, as you now know, that he had a secret weapon that worked irrespective of what the business was called. His chain of restaurants was so successful that he has since been bought out by one of the big conglomerates. They took down that sign that read "Sam's Cafe" and replaced it with one that reads "Velvet Turtle."

Recently Philip Wrigley, the son of the founder of Wrigley gum, passed away. In the story of his life there were some interesting examples of how Mr. Wrigley practiced QWC. During World War II, Wrigley could not produce enough gum to satisfy the armed forces as well as civilian demands. So he decided to sell the standard Wrigley gum to the armed services and produce a lesser quality product for civilian consumption. He insisted, however, that the name Wrigley not be used on the civilian product, and the public never associated Wrigley with the wartime substitute.

At another crucial point in his business life, Wrigley again supported QWC. The board of directors decided to lower the quality of the gum because they were experiencing cost increases. When Wrigley found himself outvoted, rather than go along with the directors he resigned as chairman of the company. His action so impressed the directors that they reversed their decision and the quality was maintained.

Another case of QWC can be seen in the company Marie Callender Pies in southern California. Starting some years ago as a modest pie shop, it made pies just the way that your mother would at home. There was no consideration given to what the pies cost (or sold for); the only goal was quality. Marie Callender began to grow in both reputation and number of stores. As they grew, they developed into a restaurant and soon included a broader luncheon and dinner menu.

They found QWC to be a powerful formula for success. It removed them from competition. Each menu item had the same secret ingredient. I have two complaints to make about Marie Callenders. Their prices are high. Also, I can never seem to get near the places; people are always waiting for three-quarters of an hour in the middle of the afternoon to have lunch. It's QWC in action.

On the other hand, I know a food operation that started with QWC, built a reputation, then multiplied. Later they lost the QWC touch. This can happen when one fellow starts a business with the magic ingredient and then sells out to another company whose managers are not familiar with the QWC principle. What took one man years to build up can be nullified in a period of weeks. The word-of-mouth wireless will be all over town before the new owners know what hit them.

What we learn here is that QWC doesn't take brains at all. It really takes more guts than brains. The professional managers who come in can be the brightest fellows around, but it is easy for them to discard the QWC formula. This particular chain is still run by professionals and has continued to expand, but now one doesn't have to wait to be seated.

These case histories are instances where quality without compromise results from the purchase of the most expensive raw materials available. QWC can be applied in other ways too. In many cases, a finished product has elements that affect its quality other than the ingredients themselves. In the doughnut business, one element that affects quality is freshness. We can use the best ingredients in the world in a product, and they will be worthless unless the product is also sold fresh.

Another example of QWC not related to ingredients is service. In some cases service becomes an important factor indeed. There is a famous dinner-house chain in California that has a great reputation for QWC. It also applies to their service. The founder of the company is known to bus tables when necessary. He dismissed his own brother-in-law for being slack in upholding the service standards.

In other words, to accomplish QWC, every single link that makes up the finished product must be treated with the same meticulous approach: without compromise. These links are all part of the makeup of the product itself, and include raw materials, freshness, service, cleanliness, and whatever other factors have a bearing on the product.

There is a large nursery in Woodland Hills, California, called Boething's that does an enormous amount of business. My wife witnessed an encounter there that gives us a hint that QWC is at work. Peggy was at the checkout area and a lady had a potted geranium she had picked out for herself. The saleslady reached over and took the plant from the customer, put it under the counter, and said, "I am sorry, but you can't have that plant." The customer, somewhat surprised, said, "Why, I picked that plant out myself." The saleslady then told her, "This geranium is far too lanky and it really shouldn't have been put out." With that, the saleslady picked out one that was a real beauty.

In every one of the success stories that results from QWC, there is a common element at work. It is word-of-mouth. Advertising is generated by the product itself. If a product is really the finest in town, word-of-mouth will be an irresistible force to propel the business upward. Keep in mind, too, that word-of-mouth is a double-edged sword. If a product is poor, word-of-mouth will result in a downward spiral so swift the operator won't ever know what hit him. He will have many excuses (the weather, the economy, etc.), and all but the right one. He was squelched by some competitor who was crazy enough to zap him with QWC.

Most of these case histories have been about the food industry. Indeed, food is extraordinarily responsive to quality. It will be up to your own ingenuity to see if this interesting ingredient has a place in your own business. Think about it. I hope it will work for you.

15
PILOT OPERATION FIRST

The expression "turkey" is used to describe a loser. No matter how farfetched or unorthodox a potential new business may seem, there is a simple technique to reduce risk of failure to just about zero: test it first. You just never know whether your idea is a turkey or a glorious winner until it is tested.

"Test a business first" is such an easy thing to say. Everyone eagerly accepts the doctrine of "pilot operation first." But the fact is there are irrepressible forces that cause both new and experienced business owners to commit their life savings to untested operations. We will discuss these forces so that you will be able to spot them.

When we look at large business operations, we see the principle of "pilot operation first" everywhere: full-scale wind tunnel testing takes place before an airplane is built; a petrochemical plant deals with controlled chemical structures, yet it is standard practice to build a pilot plant before large production units are committed.

The doctrine of "pilot operation first" can be applied to virtually any business you start:

1. If you are starting a chain operation, do not start the second unit until all features of the first one work really well, including its profitability.

2. If you are marketing a product, test-market it first, and be sure to determine how much people are willing to pay for it.

3. If you're manufacturing a product, work out every aspect of manufacture, cost, and marketability before starting production.

4. If you're getting into a service business, do not make large or long-term obligations (including a lease) until you prove the business and its profitability.

In many businesses maturing over a long period of time, the idea of testing things first is simply a part of natural evolution and growth. The classic story of someone starting small, without any money, and building an empire brick by brick implies that the business grew out of a process of experience and therefore testing.

I have a friend who is about to start a chain of coffee shops. When he talks about his plans, the pupils in his eyes dilate and he just glows with enthusiasm. There is no way anyone could deter him. This is altogether good, provided he does not fall into one of the tar pits that lurk along the start-up road that every new businessman takes. These tar pits are posted with the following sign:

> HERE, SUNK AND OUT OF SIGHT,
> ARE THE REMAINS OF
>
> _____
>
> *(fill in name)*
>
> WHO FAILED TO FOLLOW THE ROAD MAP CALLED:
>
> PILOT OPERATION FIRST

You must be aware that there are certain almost irresistible forces that will pull you away from the safe road of starting with a pilot operation. If you understand these forces, you will recognize them for what they are and not be deterred from what you know to be the safe approach. These forces can be considered as an "enemies list" of the "pilot operation first" approach.

The first enemy, and the most difficult to overcome, is self-confidence. An entrepreneur is by nature an affirmative person. Without self-confidence, not many of us would have ever elected the adventure of having our own business. However, self-confidence, like any worthwhile force, must be harnessed to produce results. Self-confidence must be incorporated into a force that is supporting the pilot operation and helping to make it work rather than becoming a force to oppose it. Never let your self-confidence permit you to skip the test-first rules.

The second enemy is your confidence in the product or service itself. Again, while this confidence is necessary, it must be used to support your belief that the product will stand the scrutiny of your pilot plant operation, rather than to excuse or omit this evaluation process.

Another terrible enemy of the "pilot operation first" concept is haste. The haste to get going. Business winners are not hasty; and surely the time you spend in testing your business is critical. Your entire business future depends on it.

Another interesting enemy is money. By this I mean too much money. If you had an absolutely unlimited amount of money to start a business, you wouldn't need a pilot operation at all. You would just keep throwing money into your operation until it worked. You and I know, however, that a person who is about to start his own business does so with a limited and usually dearly earned stake. This stake must work. You don't have another pile of money to use if the first doesn't make it work. So you test first. You make the pilot plant work, and then you're ready to commit those big dollars that have been set aside.

There is still another enemy of "pilot operation first." It might best be described as "easier said than done." So many of our plans seem so bright in concept and on paper, but the only way we can prove them is to do them. When you prove them with a pilot plant, you may find yourself with a package utterly different from the one you visualized. The function of a pilot plant is to prove that your concepts can be transformed into a viable real business.

Another enemy is a record of prior successes. A person's past success is a tribute to good judgment in other businesses, but has no bearing on whether the business at hand makes any sense or not. Abe Lincoln had a very ungainly walk which resulted in his placing each foot down carefully, with a flat-footed stance. This was a holdover from his days on the farm where any step on uncertain soil could be hazardous, in spite of each prior step being trouble-free. Step into a new business with a flat-footed stance, testing each step of the way.

A final enemy is to have a proprietary product. Some may think that because their product is unique the world will beat a path to their door. If you have a proprietary product which is so great you feel that a pilot plant operation is not needed, then remind yourself of how many Broadway plays became successful. Nothing is more proprietary than a play. Why don't they all succeed, then? Because people don't come to see them. In a business, you can prove it first. Here is the full enemies list for a pilot operation:

1. Self-confidence.
2. Confidence in the product.
3. Haste.
4. Money.
5. It is easier said than done.
6. Prior success.
7. A proprietary product.

The pilot plant approach will apply to virtually all enterprises. Surely if you're planning multiple stores you will want the first one proven before starting the second. If you're manufacturing a product, test it in the marketplace first. If you intend to furnish services, prove those services are sufficiently in demand to result in a profitable business.

In most multiple-unit businesses, multiplicity itself is a necessary ingredient for success. For example, it would obviously be difficult to build a large corporation with a single doughnut shop. But, just as clearly, a large chain of doughnut shops can become a significant company indeed. One of the tricks in a multiple-unit business is having the patience to confine operations to one store while you polish the operation and resisting the temptation to open new units in order to generate more sales. The first unit must operate alone for a long enough period to enable all kinds of problems to emerge and be dealt with. This period can be costly because only one store is operating.

It is better to cope with the problems in the first unit, including limited sales and even losses, than take the risk of adding units before the first one is adequately tested. The risk of adding additional units too soon lies in the fact that in each new unit you obligate yourself for fixed and often long-term debt, without having the source of funds (profit from the new units) proven. The problem of working with one pilot operation becomes enormously aggravated if you are working with two or more. To add additional units prematurely will risk the entire company.

Some years ago one of the leaders in food franchising, International Industries, developed a new fast-food concept called The Dog House. The building was superb. It was a small, prefabricated metal unit that could be erected and opened in thirty days, compact enough to fit onto a corner of an existing service station. The design was uniquely clever and carried the hot dog theme throughout. The stools appeared to be upholstered fire hydrants. The menu had all kinds of clever variations of hot dogs.

International Industries believed it was just too good to have to test. The concept was so outstanding in every respect that they just could not wait to apply the principle of "pilot operation first." Twenty Dog Houses sprang up throughout the Los Angeles area, all at the same time. Problems began to surface in all twenty units simultaneously. These problems were immeasurably more difficult because there were twenty times the fixed obligation of rent, fixture payments, and other unanticipated costs. The units simply could not generate enough sales to be profitable.

Had only one store opened with fatal defects they would have had one store to write off. Or, in one store, problems might have been worked out to result in one successful operation. Then they would have been in a position to multiply this success in additional stores.

In some instances it is difficult to test a new product completely. Surely a special risk factor is inherent with products in which style or public fancy plays a role. Ford Motor Company had every conceivable testing tool going for it, yet they produced one of the most celebrated turkeys of all time in the Edsel. Max Factor cosmetics encountered some hard times because one of their new fragrance lines simply did not catch on. And I think that the business of manufacturing clothing must be like a perpetual roller coaster ride.

These businesses in which style plays an important role have their own set of rules when it comes to testing procedures. I suppose there are special breeds of entrepreneurs who thrive on these risks, on the allure and excitement of the roller coaster. But for most of us, in more pedestrian businesses, the pilot operation first gives us a prudent measure of safety before we go all out.

The worst possible example of what can happen without a pilot operation first is one I can speak about with a good deal of authority, because it happened to me. It is all so clear now, but at the time I had absolutely no idea I was on the road to disaster.

The occasion was the start of the chain of Amigos restaurants. I was the leader of the bunch, and a group of us had spent a couple of years planning every detail of the operation of the first Amigos. And what an operation it was! It was a beautiful restaurant in Costa Mesa, California, and had an enthusiastic public lining up at the doors to try it out. Our confidence in the Amigos concept was so great that five other locations were built within the year after the first one opened.

Amigos just didn't work. In the final judgment of public opinion, it was not a good restaurant. I suddenly realized that we had wandered off into the tar pits. We didn't have one pilot plant to make work; we had six of them. We had an unmanageable bucket of worms to straighten out that ultimately had to be solved by converting all six of the restaurants to an entirely different kind of operation which also failed later.

Those harsh memories are dulled somewhat now by the intervening years. But as the pain has subsided, the management errors come into better focus and they toll out like sad, wise bells that all can hear. I failed to start with a pilot operation first. Why did I overlook this? Here are the reasons:

1. Self-confidence.
2. Confidence in the product (the concept).
3. We were all in too much of a hurry.
4. Money: it is too bad that we didn't have less to

spend. If we had enough for only one restaurant, we wouldn't have started the other franchised units prematurely.

5. It is easier said than done. No one could make us believe that the restaurant business was one for experienced professionals.

6. I had never had a flop before. Famous last words.

7. We believed that the Amigos idea was so special (proprietary) there was simply no thought given to the possibility of its not working.

Now for a winner: how Kresge's entered the discount department store field. The discount store industry started in New England, and it grew rapidly. Most of the early chains were the result of entrepreneurs who were pioneers in the discount approach to merchandising, and who wrote the book as they grew.

When Kresge decided to enter the field, they did not have the sense of urgency that prevails in so many start-up companies. Kresge's approach was to have a pilot operation first. To begin, they compiled all of the do's and don'ts they could glean from discount competitors. The concept was based on this input plus their own know-how.

Once the concept was fully designed, they picked a representative marketing area and opened one store. This single store operated for many months. During this time a number of things happened. First, problems emerged and were handled. Also, emphasis on different areas of the business was modified, based on experience. A complete operations manual with procedures was established. Finally the store became a great success. This was the start of K-Mart, one of the bright successes of retailing history in America. The multiplication of one successful pilot plant resulted in the second largest retailer in the country.

Winners test first and then multiply their successful pilots. Earl Scheib did it in car painting. Mrs. See's did it in candy.

McDonald's did it in hamburgers. One after another, the stories of winners show the same approach: figure it out first with a pilot operation and then proliferate it.

16

H.B.S., I LOVE YOU

It's nice to be associated with professionals. In business, one password that identifies you as a professional is "H.B.S."

In California we have beautiful Palm Springs. Its residents let others know where they are from with a classic bumper sticker: "P.S. I LOVE YOU."

H.B.S. has a special meaning in business, and in business too it's nice to let others know where you are from. While the Harvard Business School is one of many fine graduate schools, none of which I attended, it will serve as the symbol for my theme. Any person who wants his own business should aim for a master's degree from the best graduate school of business available to him.

A certain sequence should take place. First, learn the fundamentals of business management. Second, decide upon your business (you may already have done this before your first step). Third, work for someone else who is in "your" business.

Let's look at each step in more detail. First, learning the fundamentals of business management. If you are a young person with college still ahead of you, train for business management. Unless your chosen business (if indeed you have chosen one at all yet) is one requiring specialized undergraduate study such as engineering, consider business administration as your college major. Then aim for an M.B.A. in a graduate school of business. If your business goal does require a specialty, then business administration could be taken as a minor, again with the goal of qualifying for a graduate school of business.

The more formal schooling you receive, particularly graduate work, the higher are your chances for success. Graduate business schools follow the case study method, which becomes a practical education in dealing with the pragmatics as well as the theories of business management.

If you are beyond the age of planning a traditional university education, there are still avenues for accomplishing the first step. One possibility is to go back to school. Or enroll in the best university extension course in business management that is available. An increasing variety of business courses are offered by university extension facilities. You can choose a combination of subjects that will add to your confidence and sophistication. Set your own speed by taking as heavy or light a study load as will suit your schedule.

The second step is to decide on your business. You have a lot of time to make this decision. If a person has not decided on a business before entering formal business education, it is perfectly all right. The period of formal education can be used for pondering this decision. You can make the decision by the time you leave graduate school.

The third step is to work for someone else who is in "your" business. This vocational training that follows your formal education is important for two reasons. First, it will act as your internship. It will give you a chance to learn your business and to experience its idiosyncrasies. Also, it will give you an opportunity to save money, because you are going to need some seed capital. Perhaps it will not be possible to get the overall picture by working for one firm. Work for two or three or whatever it takes to gain experience in all aspects of your business. You now have the enormous advantage of the formal education, coupled with the practical education gained by working for someone else.

The fourth step is to do it. Your education is now complete. You are prepared in theory, in practice, and have the capital saved.

I've never been to business school, but have observed the advantages that come to those who have. My partner, Frank Watase, graduated from the Harvard Graduate School of Business. There is no question that H.B.S. enormously expanded Frank's capability and opportunity. The H.B.S. diploma was his ticket to the finest employment opportunity and he used it to gain the best work experience.

Those who go through graduate business schools are professionals:

> **1.** They can discuss a financial statement like a pro.
>
> **2.** They do not get buried by trivia. They keep a long and broad view of their business, because their training helps them to contend with substantive business problems. They don't count the ants while the elephants march by.
>
> **3.** They can communicate better in the important relationships that a business owner must maintain: with bankers, CPAs, lawyers, and customers.
>
> **4.** A graduate business degree adds credibility when dealing with bankers or other financial sources. Remember, money provides the fuel necessary to make a business function, and the ability to communicate expertly about money matters will be very important to you.

I must acknowledge that graduate school training is not appropriate for everyone. There are business objectives that can be achieved without business school. However, most of us are underachievers because we do not fully nourish our potential. Education will improve our performance. Therefore, the ultimate educational possibilities we can experience should be pursued. Perhaps it is inappropriate to consider business school training for yourself, but if you have a son or daughter who may go into his or her own business, encourage him to go on to graduate school.

When you are the head of a business, you are in the big leagues. To be, and stay, in the big leagues you must be a professional. To be a professional, exercise every advantage of education you can muster.

17
SHALL I FRANCHISE?

There seems to be a widespread belief that the way for a small company to achieve rapid expansion is to franchise, or sell the right to an individual or group to market one's product or service. There are some franchise operations, especially in the fast-food industry, that have indeed grown spectacularly.

The fact is that franchising is not the only way to achieve a high rate of expansion. This chapter will review both sides of franchising, with emphasis on some of the pitfalls. You may come to the conclusion that franchising your business would be like starting with the wrong shirt button: you could end up with a mess when you get to the top. Let's first look at the background of franchising.

During the late 1960s there was a proliferation of franchise deals. It was a time when hundreds of companies, most of them fast-food operations, began making them. Franchising was the key to success for small private enterprises, and there was a great bull market in their publicly held stocks. There were even instances in which franchisees (buyers of fran chises) that had grown into multiple-store chains sold public offerings of stock.

The business journals touted getting a franchise as the answer for individuals who wanted to be in business but who did not have the necessary experience. Franchisees could become associated with franchisers who did have the know-how and who would be their "big brother" to get them started and guide them after they were established.

This is a good example of the gulf that can exist between concept and reality. In concept, franchising has some sensible points, both for the franchiser and the franchisee. In the light and experience of reality, however, franchising can become a bitter disappointment for both.

A few well-managed companies have overcome franchising problems by the sheer success of their operations. McDonald's, of course, is one great example. Others have switched from franchising their stores to running company-owned stores. McDonald's is a good example of this too, since they have repurchased many franchise stores. Denny's, the coffee shop chain, switched completely from franchising to company-operated stores.

Winchell Donuts (a division of Denny's) switched 500 franchised doughnut shops overnight into company-operated shops. They offered their franchisees one of two alternatives. One choice was to stay on as managers and receive certain fringe benefits which as franchisees they were not getting, plus the same income potential they had as franchisees. The other choice was for the franchisees to leave, and be reimbursed their franchise deposits.

After the switch, Winchell has grown on a much more stable basis. As a franchiser, they were headed down the spiral of class-action lawsuits and loss of control of their operations.

On the other hand, there are a number of franchise operations that are still going strong today. They all have some interesting common traits. First, the franchisers are very large firms. Second, the franchisees are usually substantial and profitable. Finally, the franchisees have a large investment in their franchise operations. Car dealerships and Coca-Cola franchised bottlers are the type that work best today.

Let's review some of the attractions of franchising as far as the franchiser is concerned. First, it is not difficult to sell franchises if your business works. Because of abuses, both state and federal agencies now carefully control the sale of franchises. Assuming you have sold one (legally), you now have a lot of cash. This is franchise income to you, after you have subtracted the costs of putting your franchisee into business.

Your franchisee, who has put up a lot of his money, is now ready to run his store. He is well motivated to do a good job. For him it will be swim or drown, so he is going to do a little swimming. All of these factors are pluses for the franchiser: ease of selling, cash in the bank, and a highly motivated franchisee. Terrific.

Yum Yum Donut Shops is frequently approached by people with fists full of money who want to buy a franchise. With the number of operating stores we now have (ninety), we could franchise each and every one, and in one swoop take in at least $5,000,000. Now, that seems appealing, doesn't it? The fact is that it would not make good business sense at all. The underlying difficulty is that we might find ourselves left with nothing. Remember, a company runs like an oil refinery. It is either in control or out of control. If an oil refinery operates out of control, you simply do not know what is going to come out of the pipeline.

If we were to franchise our doughnut shops, we would have ninety franchisees, each with a proprietary interest in his store. We would be dealing with ninety partners, each of whom would have a very strong opinion and voice. Remember, their life savings may be on the line. Each one would be without experience, but in most cases would have their own ideas on how their store should be run. These beliefs usually conflict with experienced operating know-how.

Perhaps General Motors can, but you cannot control a franchisee. However, for the sake of argument, let us assume you could. You are in a game you cannot win. If the store does well, you will not be able to take a fair profit from it and still have a franchisee who is making enough to be happy. You will not be able to take the income you could in a company-owned operation. This explains why McDonald's and Denny's are either buying back franchises or opening new stores as company units. So, even if the store does well, you lose. Your earnings in relation to your operating costs, investment, know-how, and enormous rent liability will simply not be great enough to make it worthwhile.

That is how bad it is when you win. Now let me tell you how bad it is when the store is a turkey. If you have a franchised store that does poorly for any reason (including a recalcitrant franchisee), two things will happen: the franchisee will stop paying the rent and he will sue you for fraud. And of course, other things can happen too. The losing business gets worse and worse. When we have a company store that does poorly, since we control the store, we will do whatever it takes to make it successful, and we have done this in a number of cases. Not so with a franchisee. All we would have is a closed building, long-term fixed obligations on rent and equipment, a tarnished image, and a lawsuit.

One of the reasons that companies get into franchising is that it is hard to say no when someone offers a bundle of money to buy a franchise. If you have a going business that works and is suitable for more outlets, you can be sure these offers will be made. This temptation is hard to resist, especially if you are short of working capital (which is a normal situation for a young and growing firm). Submitting to such offers could be an easy way to convert a growing business into your own private hell.

Once a company has submitted to the lure of selling franchises, it becomes susceptible to compromising on new store locations. The franchiser is usually under pressure to satisfy the appetites of franchisees who are throwing money at him. If you own your stores, you will use a greater degree of selectivity in new locations. You simply pass the dice on a questionable location and let someone else take a chance. Some franchiser who has a franchisee barking at him for a location will take it.

Here is a summary of problems you would face in franchising your business:

1. You will have to deal with unknowledgeable franchisees.
2. You will not be able to exercise absolute control over your business.
3. If a franchisee does well, you still cannot make enough to give a fair return on your risks and investment.
4. If a franchisee does poorly, you have a cash drain and a lawsuit.
5. You will be controlled by governmental agencies, both state and federal, that you haven't even heard of yet.
6. Your bankers, suppliers, and landlords will question your credibility.
7. You may never be able to manufacture your own products for sale through your own retail stores. With a franchisee it's "restraint of trade."
8. You will find yourself taking secondary locations.

There is a further conclusion you can draw. Since it might be bad news to become a franchiser, it might not be such a great idea to become a franchisee either. There are some luring temptations for someone who wants to become an entrepreneur to consider buying a franchise. Again, the conceptual advantages are impressive. One of the greatest inducements is that the business has already been proven. Also, you will be your own boss, and yet will be operating within the sheltered protection of the parent company's strength and expertise. It would seem like having your own business, and yet not taking risks.

Well, many, many franchisees lose their savings in ill-conceived deals, including ones in which the parent companies go rolling right along, reselling the turkey to someone else. In order for a franchise to work, the operation and follow-through must be so meticulously adhered to that the franchisee becomes something of a robot. The successful franchise operations are the ones in which the franchiser's continuation fees are high enough to result in the franchisee's having to work very hard to keep afloat.

If you like the operation of a franchised company, it would make more sense to learn everything about it, then do it yourself. First, you must identify the critical elements that make the business work. Let's look at an example. There is a franchised chain of ice cream stores that is enormously successful, if you judge by the number of operating stores. Franchisees must work hard to make money in these stores. The operation has some important elements:

1. A large variety of premium-quality ice cream.
2. No products other than ice cream are sold.
3. Great merchandising.
4. Beautiful decor and interiors.
5. Widespread recognition.

Now, let's assume you are interested in opening an ice cream store. The trick will be to discipline yourself to stick to the critical elements that made the proven chain successful and not to deviate. In this case, selling sandwiches would be a deviation.

To start a successful business, it is not necessary (or even advisable) that you create a new product or concept. If you like a certain business, including one that is franchised, learn about it and then do it yourself. In this example, you will not have widespread recognition going for you. You will create it by word-of-mouth, advertising, and an outstanding operation.

You can't win in business today unless you have a well-controlled operation. As a franchiser, you cannot be in complete control, and even if you could it would not be worth it. As a franchisee, you still can lose it all, and if you are one of the fortunate ones who are successful, you can ultimately become very tired. Consider these points before deciding on a franchising concept, either as a franchiser or as a franchisee.

18
KEEP SCORE

This may seem farfetched, but could you imagine playing tennis year after year and never knowing how to keep score? It happens all the time in business. An incredible number of businessmen will clump through a career and never know what the score is.

The score is kept by balance sheets and profit and loss (P&L) statements. If you consider how much of your life will be spent in business, you can afford to spend a great deal of effort to learn accounting.

The chances are that as a start-up businessman, you are not adequately trained in accounting, yet accounting and bookkeeping will be the tools to keep your business in control. To remedy this, you must learn accounting by going to school: high schools, junior colleges, and universities all have classes in bookkeeping and accounting. There are no short cuts. This is an absolute prerequisite for any starting business person.

You're not going to learn accounting by having someone else do it for you. You have only one alternative, to go into overdrive. "Overdrive" means extra effort. You're going to have to give up some TV or other pleasures to acquire this knowledge. Only when you have completed comprehensive courses in bookkeeping and accounting, which go all the way through the complete financial report, will you be ready.

Learning accounting will enable you to self-diagnose the condition of your business. Like a doctor using an EKG and a blood-pressure reading to evaluate and remedy a patient's condition, you will have your balance sheet, P&L statement, and cash flow to prescribe treatment. You will act as your own physician to maintain business health.

I recommend this step-by-step plan of attack:

Step One: Go to school and get formal accounting training. Continue your schooling until you are able to prepare and analyze financial statements. Without this training, you will be at the wheel of an enlarging and accelerating business and be driving with blinders on, because you will not know where you are or where you are going.

Step Two: Line up a CPA before you start your business. Have his help from the very beginning. There will be multiple contributions he can make in your initial start-up process. Have him help set up your books and your complete accounting procedures.

Don't settle for anyone without the CPA credential. You will probably want to start with a small firm and possibly even a one-man office. Explain to your new CPA that you personally will be keeping the books and making the reports for the initial stage of your business.

Step Three: In the start-up period, being your own bookkeeper will make you intimately familiar with the procedures. You will learn by experience, and will save the expense of a bookkeeper. Do it all yourself. Pull off the weekly or monthly financial statements, including balance sheet and P&L statement. Prepare your own cash flow projections. Prepare the quarterly returns yourself. Your CPA can check your work to be sure you are doing it correctly. Get him involved as your consultant in financial matters.

Step Four: When you really have the hang of it, turn over your books to a bookkeeper. By now you will be so familiar with your bookkeeping that delegation is appropriate. Here are some rules I have found helpful in keeping score:

Take the pulse of your business at frequent intervals. On a store level, pull off an income statement every week. As described in Chapter 25, this weekly P&L can also be used as a basis for a manager bonus system. Prepare company financial statements monthly. Frequent financial reports will help you remedy problems while they are still subject to correction. If a ship is veering off course, the earlier you correct it the smaller the deviation will be. In business, many problems simply cannot be corrected months after the event occurs; you cannot turn back the clock to regain what has been lost.

Another reason for monthly statements is to be sure books are kept current. Without monthly statements, which require that books and bank account reconciliations be current, you would be surprised how easy it is to let bookkeeping get behind. Like physical examinations, it seems to be a postponable activity.

Start off with a manual system of bookkeeping. Computer systems can come later when you find compelling reasons to switch. For example, when your payroll reaches a large number, you might first consider a payroll computer service, rather than switching your entire accounting system.

When your CPA starts, ask him to prepare a written list of recommendations for internal controls. This list might include certain equipment recommendations, such as the use of a locked fireproof file cabinet for important files. It might also include certain procedures and audit controls to minimize the risks of dishonesty in personnel, not only in your bookkeeping functions, but also in all company operations. With each year-end audit, ask your CPA to give you a report of recommended changes or additions to your accounting procedures and internal controls.

As soon as you can afford it, have your CPA give you a certified statement. In order to do this, he will go through additional audit procedures, increasing his time and therefore the cost of the audit. However, a certified statement has such great credibility in the finance world that it can be a sound investment. The thoroughness of a certified statement can also uncover accounting inaccuracies. It is like paying for the super-thorough physical examination, which can give you greater assurance of your health.

Your books must reflect reality. Never play games with your financial statements for the purpose of making your financial condition look better than it is. The only way you will ever build the confidence of people like your banker who rely on your financial statements is to have them see reality in your reports.

While your statements must be absolutely honest, you should still take advantage of every rule you can in order to minimize or defer the impact of income taxes on your corporate earnings. Your cash flow will be the fuel to strengthen and enlarge your business. It comes from only two sources: noncash expenses (such as depreciation) and after-tax income. "After tax" depends, obviously, on how much income tax you must pay. This can vary depending on how thoroughly you take advantage of acceptable methods of reducing or deferring taxes, such as accelerated depreciation or investment tax credits.

Operate on budgets, and have your managers operate on them too. If your business requires long-distance telephone calls, then have everyone accountable for telephone expense, which becomes part of their budget. People will watch expenses when they operate on budgets. Only the very rich can live without them, and you surely shouldn't run a business without one.

Compartmentalize responsibilities so that each department has its own separate budget. For example, our maintenance department is responsible for keeping the stores in good working order. Until this department was given a budget, it was difficult to predict what maintenance costs would be each month. Now, with a budget, our maintenance costs are controlled and also significantly reduced.

Don't delegate authority to sign checks. This is your ultimate control over what is spent. If you issue a lot of checks, use a check protector, which imprints the amount to be paid on the check.

Be watchful of key percentages in your P&L. In our business, there are two crucial items: purchases and labor cost. If one or both of these are not within acceptable limits, then the bottom line of profit will not work. Critical percentages can reveal a multitude of problems. If purchases are unusually high, it might indicate overordering, overproduction or possibly employee dishonesty. If you are preparing frequent P&Ls, an immediate remedy can be applied.

Unfortunately, dishonesty is a significant fact of life in almost any business. Dishonesty can occur in employees, customers, suppliers, or even from outright robbery. Different businesses will have different exposures to these losses. Also, each business has its own most successful way to control dishonesty. You should learn what the risks are for your business and be familiar with the most successful tools to combat them. See how those already in your kind of business handle dishonesty.

For example, let's assume you want to open (heaven forbid) a doughnut shop. By talking to operators, you could learn what their risks are and how to control them. In such a shop a salesclerk may not ring up sales and later simply pocket the money. This can be controlled in a number of ways, including taking inventory before and after the shift, and by cash control procedures.

Whenever you do suspect or encounter dishonesty, you must be very careful how you handle it. You can be subject to substantial lawsuits through intemperate accusations. Consult your lawyer on handling employee dishonesty. Have a clearcut policy that is approved by your lawyer. Use your accountant to design controls to discourage thefts of all kinds.

Never misuse funds that you hold in trust accounts such as payroll taxes that have been withheld from wages. Always make these payments on time. IRS agents can and do padlock the doors of business owners who misuse the money that has been withheld from paychecks for income taxes and social security. State and federal tax agents will "pierce the corporate veil" and collect withheld taxes from corporate officers.

Have an employee benefit package. Develop a written policy on vacations, holidays, hours, and general employment rules. Perhaps you will want to give employees a day off on their birthday. You may want to initiate a group health insurance program, which will become a part of your employee benefit package. You should attract and keep good people, and you will be competing with larger companies that have strong benefit programs.

Keep abreast of key ratios in your balance sheet; one in particular is your current ratio. This is as vital as your heartbeat. It will tell you if you can service your short-term debt.

In addition to your financial statements, cash flow management will keep your operation in control. Chapter 19 explains how to use cash flow control.

Once your business is rolling, comparing current weekly or monthly sales to the same period a year ago becomes helpful. It gives you a fast indicator of performance and problems. If a store is doing less than it did in the same period a year ago, a red light should flash. You should be able to account for the drop in sales: it might be new competition or it might be poor operations.

There are a number of other benefits gained from direct experience in accounting. You will be conversant with the language of people who are important to you: your banker, suppliers, and even customers. A banker will have confidence in dealing with a borrower who is sophisticated in financial reports. When you get into the big leagues, you'll be dealing more and more with balance sheets and income statements, and less with the day-to-day operations. You will need to expertly interpret financial statements of other companies. This knowledge will enable you to be informed about competition, suppliers, and customers.

A comprehensive knowledge of accounting, then, is an important prerequisite to going into business. You will be in business to win. How will you know you are winning if you can't keep score?

19
CASH FLOW

A helicopter once crashed in Los Angeles and took the lives of the pilot and a passenger. It was a clear day. The helicopter had been functioning perfectly. The pilot was an expert, with thousands of hours of experience. The problem was that they ran out of gas.

Cash is to your business what gas was to that helicopter. A smoothly running business with experienced ownership will cease to exist anytime payroll checks cannot be cashed. The management of money, which is business fuel, is essential for the survival of a business. Any individual who does not have the skill of managing cash has no place in business ownership.

The management of business fuel is cash flow control. This chapter will teach you all you need to know. However, if this subject bores you, stop and think again about whether you want your own business. If you cannot understand cash flow, your chances of sharing the fate of the helicopter are just too great.

Cash flow is to a business what oxygen is to a person. We will cease to exist when we are deprived of oxygen. A business will cease to exist when it is deprived of cash. A business is sustained by its own form of breathing, which is liquidity. "Liquidity" means having cash in the bank to pay obligations within every consecutive, ongoing period of time. The time periods can be calculated either by the week or by the month. The moment a business does not have cash, its checks will bounce at the bank, and the business will check out of existence.

Cash flow control gives you an accurate measurement right now of your future liquidity. Cash flow procedure, by predicting and controlling future liquidity, becomes an invaluable tool.

First, you must understand the difference between liquidity and making money. They are not the same, although each will have an effect on the other. Any business that is losing money will ultimately fail, because the loss of money will ultimately strangle liquidity, and the business will finally run out of cash.

A business that is making money can also fail if its ability to stay liquid is not controlled. Remember that liquidity equals cash. You can be making money hand over fist, but if what you make is not in the form of cash, you cannot write payroll checks. For example, profits in the form of receivables won't pay the rent.

Cash flow, purely from an accounting definition, means net profit plus noncash expenses. It is the amount of cash which you have available at the end of an accounting period. A good example of a noncash expense is depreciation. You charge depreciation as an expense, but it is a noncash expense, and therefore it is available and in your bank account.

Your job will be to control your cash flow. You cannot afford to play guessing games when it comes to liquidity. The technique you will learn here will eliminate uncertainty regarding future liquidity: you will be able to predict and control it. First, let's consider the elements that have a bearing on future liquidity, shown in Table 1.

As you see in Table 1, the format provides a weekly analysis of cash flow. For some businesses this could be done in monthly periods. The columns on the left and right indicate "in" and "out." These are estimated figures, with the exception of the starting cash for the first week. After that, you are dealing with the future and, therefore, projections.

The steps in preparing a cash flow control are as follows. The first element is "Starting cash" for the very first week. The second element will be the items that make up cash income: all of the sources of cash during each period, including cash sales, cash from other sources such as borrowing, receivables that are paid, and any others. The elements of "out" appear on the right side of the form, and are a breakdown of expenses that result in cash being paid out during the same

TABLE 1
CASH FLOW CONTROL

WEEK ENDING: __March 1__

IN		ACTUAL		OUT	
Starting cash	1000	____	____	Payroll	300
Sales	1000	____	____	Purchases	400
Other	—	____	____	Payroll taxes	100
Total in	2000	____	____	Checklist Exhibit B (utilities)	100
Less: total out	900	____	____	Total out	900
Balance	1100	____	____		

WEEK ENDING: __March 8__

IN		ACTUAL		OUT	
Starting cash	1100	____	____	Payroll	____
Sales	____	____	____	Purchases	____
Other	____	____	____	Payroll taxes	____
Total in		____	____	Checklist Exhibit B	____
Less: total out	____	____	____	Total out	____
Balance	____	____	____		

period. The "Balance" is the meaningful number. It appears as the last item of the "in" column, after the "Total out" has been subtracted from the "Total in." This final "Balance" for the period will tell you whether you have a positive or a negative bank balance.

The "Balance" of the first period then becomes the "Starting cash" of the second period. Since the "Balance" of one week becomes the "Starting cash" of the next week, each week must be completed to determine its "Balance" before the subsequent week's "Starting cash" can be entered.

The further you project into the future, the less reliable your estimates will be, because errors become cumulative as they are carried forward from one week into the next one. If you are using a weekly analysis, plan about eight weeks at a time.

Now you can design a cash flow for your own business. Prepare the format for each page, including everything in Table 1 except the figures. Then insert the "Starting cash" for the first week of your analysis, your beginning cash on hand.

Now, fill in the other numbers by category. First, forecast the cash from sales for each week in the projection. If you have an entirely cash business, the "Sales" will be the sales forecast for each week. If you have a business that sells on credit, show when money is received from sales, not when the sale itself is made. For example, if your sales are made on terms of net thirty days, the cash will not be shown until thirty days after the sale is made, assuming customers pay on time. If there are any sources of cash other than sales, insert these numbers in the appropriate weeks.

Next, fill in the figures under the heading of "Out," dollars to be spent during the same eight-week period. First you should break down the major categories of outgoing cash, those items you know will definitely be spent. They are:

1. Payroll.
2. Cash paid for purchases.
3. Payroll taxes.

To be certain all "out" payments are included, prepare a

checklist of all items that apply to your business. This will assure that you have not inadvertently omitted items of cash outlay. Table 2 provides a sample list.

TABLE 2
CHECKLIST OF "OUT" ITEMS

Item	Due Date	Amount
Payroll	weekly	300
Purchases	weekly	400
Payroll taxes	weekly	100
Telephone	15th	50
Utilities	1st	100
Quarterly taxes	4/30, 7/30, 10/30, 1/30	350
Rent	30th	500
Insurance	15th	120
Bank interest	5th	150
Petty cash	var.	var.
Miscellaneous	var.	var.
Equipment payment	20th	160

Certain payments are periodic but not necessarily weekly, such as rent payments. So, for the purpose of cash flow control, the "out" item of rent will occur only during the last week of the month. Other "out" items also occur monthly rather than weekly, such as insurance payments, loan payments, and utility payments. Some payments may occur only in longer intervals: for example, quarterly tax payments, sales tax payments, and workmen's compensation insurance payments.

Under "out" you will enter all categories of cash outlays for each week and verify them with your checklist. For your first week of the projection, total all of the items under "in," including "Starting cash," to give you the "Total in." Next, add up all of the "out" items for the first week.

In the Cash Flow Control column under "in," you will find the item "Less: total out." This is the sum of the "out" items for that week, taken from the right side total of the "out" column. Subtract the "Less: total out" from the "Total in" and you will have the balance of cash at the end of the week. This is simple, isn't it? You start with so much cash at the beginning of the week, you add to it the cash that has come in during the week, and then you deduct the cash spent during the week to determine the cash left at the end of the week.

The cash "Balance" at the end of the first week becomes the "Starting cash" at the beginning of the second week. Now you are dealing with numbers that are all forecasts, and you repeat the process for each subsequent week until you get to the balance for each week of your eight-week period. This "Balance" for each week is your forecast bank balance. A negative balance at the end of one week becomes a negative "Starting cash" under the "in" column of the following week.

You now have completed an eight-week cash flow. Here is where the element of "control" becomes meaningful. Let's assume the "Balance" for week number six is negative. This means that at the end of the sixth week your checks are going to bounce. Now is the time, six weeks before the impending disaster, to take some form of remedial action.

There are only two solutions, both of them extremely potent. You can either increase "in" items during the six weeks prior to that fateful day, or you can decrease "out" items. One way of increasing "in" is to borrow money. Another way to increase "in" is to get in money that may be overdue from customers. Another solution is to reduce "out" items for the six-week period, in any way you can. If worse comes to worst, don't pay the rent on time. It is better to have an unhappy landlord than to have your payroll checks bounce. This is a harsh example, but I am addressing a harsh situation. You must take whatever action you deem appropriate in the "in" or "out" columns to maintain liquidity.

To a limited degree, businesses can function with a negative balance. In our doughnut shops we could operate at a minus balance figure of approximately one week's sales. The reason for this is "float." When we write a check, there is a lag of time before the check reaches our bank. For a conservative approach to cash flow, I suggest you assume that when a check is written it is instantly cashed and therefore out of your cash flow.

In the center of the Cash Flow Control form in Table 1 is the heading "Actual" for each week. Remember, we have been dealing with projected figures. As each week elapses, you enter the actual figures for each item of "in" and "out" on this part of the form. The actual "in" figures go to the left side of the center line, and the actual "out" figures go to the right of it. Then you can arrive at the actual cash flow for that week. The actual balance figure can then be carried forward to the "actual" column of the next week so you can convert each future week from a projection to an actual cash flow.

So far we have been applying cash flow control to a short-term projection of eight weeks. You now understand the essence of cash flow control, which is to forecast cash in and cash out for future intervals so as to determine future liquidity.

Another cash flow, in a different form, can also be used for long-range projections of twelve months. Table 3 follows the same rule: cash balance for one period becomes the starting cash for the next period.

Table 3 shows a business starting with $1000, and building up cash for the first two months. Then in the third month, there is a distortion of cash when $1000 is spent for a capital expense (say a piece of production equipment). This results in a minus cash balance for the months of March and April.

In October there is another distortion, the $4000 for another capital expense. This really bends cash out of shape because we end up October with a minus $2100. This projection is what your banker needs to supply your financing for those two capital purchases. Perhaps the first one in March

TABLE 3
CASH FLOW CONTROL (LONG-RANGE)

	JAN	FEB	MAR	APR	MAY	JUN	JLY	AUG	SEP	OCT	NOV	DEC
STARTING CASH	1000	1200	900	(300)	(100)	200	550	850	1200	1550	(2100)	(1800)
IN												
Sales	1000	1100	1200	1300	1300	1400	1400	1500	1500	1500	1500	1600
Total in	2000	2300	2100	1000	1200	1600	1950	2350	2700	3050	(600)	(200)
OUT												
Payroll	300	500	600	400	400	450	450	450	450	450	450	450
Purchases	300	400	400	400	300	300	300	350	350	350	350	400
Overhead	200	500	400	300	300	300	350	350	350	350	400	400
Capital expense	0	0	1000	0	0	0	0	0	0	4000	0	0
Total out	800	1400	2400	1100	1000	1050	1100	1150	1150	5150	1200	1250
CASH BALANCE (starting cash plus "in" minus "out")	1200	900	(300)	(100)	200	550	850	1200	1550	(2100)	(1800)	(1450)

should be handled by a short-term six-month loan. The larger purchase in October might be financed over a longer period of a year. Obviously, you will not want to make these purchases until you have been assured of financing. You can now begin to appreciate that there is a special advantage in maintaining good cash flow control. It will be the most important tool you have with your banker. It tells him you are trained in maintaining liquidity. After all, this is what he is most interested in too: whether your business is stable or whether it risks running out of gas. He needs cash flow projections to lend you money as much as you need it to stay alive. In addition to assuring the banker of your liquidity, your cash flow also shows him how his loan is going to be repaid. He will want to see your long-range cash flow projection as well as your short-term one.

Cash flow control can mean survival when you establish your first beachhead. It will particularly apply where sales are made on a credit basis—you sell a product today and collect the money in the future. The future could mean thirty days, or even a longer period of time.

I have previously mentioned Bob Silvers and Ben Garfinkle, who started a direct sales company. Their product sold for $300, with a low down payment and installment payments over twelve months. Salesmen were paid a large commission at the time the sale was made.

Bob and Ben were very good at selling their merchandise. Their problem was that the more they sold, the worse their cash flow became. Under "in" was a meager down payment for each sale. Under "out" was the large commission, plus the cost of the merchandise. They were so good at selling that while the business was enormously profitable, they almost sold themselves right out of existence. The only way they survived was in finally visualizing what would come in a cash flow projection. They were lucky to be able to sell stock to friends and to obtain bank loans. These sources of cash covered their negative cash flow, which went on for many months until the company reached equilibrium.

Before you even start a business, you must know what

your maximum requirement for cash will be. Surely Eisenhower wouldn't have undertaken the Normandy invasion if 1,000,000 men were needed and only 500,000 were available. It would be silly to start up a business with $10,000, only to learn after you started that $25,000 is required.

The long-range form of cash flow control (Table 3) will determine the total capital required to start. The capital required will be equal to the maximum negative "cash balance" shown on your projection in Table 3. If your projection shows a maximum negative cash flow that is greater than the capital you have planned to commit, then go back to the drawing board and restructure your approach. A great number of elements can be changed. You might need investor capital, or accounts-receivable financing. Perhaps your time frame will be longer, to achieve growth goals. Each "in" and "out" item is subject to restructuring. You manipulate and massage your projection until your plan of attack shows a positive cash flow. Use safety factors in making your forecasts. Permit your prudence to overrule your natural optimism in making estimates.

There is a human tendency to be optimistic about "in" items and to understate "out" items. The way to offset this is to be conservative on the items of cash in, and to use a very heavy pencil on the estimates of cash out. Conservative estimates will result in a more realistic approach.

Preparing a projection of cash flow can be an exciting game. The suspense lies in how the balance figures turn out after all the numbers have been entered. You may be in for some interesting surprises, such as the discovery that eight weeks hence you are going to be gloriously liquid. Or perhaps you will find a negative figure that will need creative action. Then, after cash flow has been prepared, it is fascinating to see it unfold, and to control it so as to maintain your liquidity.

A prudent person must use cash flow control in his business, especially in a start-up situation. Cash flow control will be one of the keys to your success, to determine capital needs and to preserve your liquidity.

20
LEARN FROM OTHERS

Long ago in the Swiss Alps there was a high village. It was so high that villagers kept falling off the mountaintop. Finally the mayor realized something had to be done. His solution was to build a hospital to take care of all of those who were injured. But people still were falling. Later a new mayor came into office, and felt the problem should be looked into again. His solution was to build a fence around the dangerous precipice. From that time on, villagers lived safely and happily.

The first mayor was a poor one and the second mayor was a good one. This chapter will examine the profiles of good and bad business people. From these case histories you can identify the traits of each group. Knowing what makes good and bad entrepreneurs will help you to emulate the good ones and avoid the ways of the bad ones. You will learn from others.

Business know-how is born of good and bad experiences. You can start up a business armed with the experiences of others who have already plowed the field. The case histories that follow are all true, although some names have been changed. In every case, the person was in business for himself. You will be able to identify the traits that contributed to their success or failure. At the end of the chapter the traits of the successful and the unsuccessful are listed, giving you two composite profiles, one to emulate and one to avoid like the plague.

The first winner is Joe Hirsch, owner of Hirsch Pipe and Supply Company in Los Angeles, a wholesale plumbing supply business. Joe has always done well in a field with intense competition and price cutting. Years ago, I sold Transite pipe for Johns-Manville. Joe was one of my best customers, yet he never offered discounts when he sold to plumbing contractors.

Joe's secret was that he always had a complete stock of merchandise. When I called on Joe for a Transite pipe order, he would spend an hour in the yard checking the stock of every fitting in every size. Other wholesalers took five or ten minutes to work up an order of fast sellers and concentrated on these, but Joe would painstakingly be sure his stock included every item in our catalog.

Whenever a plumber went to Hirsch Pipe and Supply, he knew that whatever he needed was there, and he would pay the extra 10 or 15 percent. Joe Hirsch did not win the game by accident. He had a preliminary plan and simply followed it through to success. His goals were: 1. Always have a complete stock. 2. Don't cut the price.

Joe's ability to operate successfully was evident in other ways. He followed through with good service; customers were waited on quickly and efficiently. Also, Joe had a knack for keeping good employees. Some of them had been with him for many years. Joe worked hard, but not overly hard. He took long summer vacations in remote parts of the world, and everything ran just as smoothly when he was gone. He has always been one I have admired as a successful businessman.

Another successful businessman was an eccentric and fabulously successful tycoon, the late Vernon Rudolph, founder and driving force of Krispy Kreme Doughnut Corporation of Winston-Salem, North Carolina. Vernon started a doughnut shop in Winston-Salem in 1937. He built the company to sales of $1,000,000 per week by 1970. It was enormously successful and profitable. By the time of his death in 1973, Krispy Kreme controlled the doughnut industry from Washington, D.C., to Florida. His company dominated the wholesale doughnut business, retail shops, manufacture of automatic equipment, and the sale of doughnut ingredients and machinery to large bakeries.

As Krispy Kreme grew into a giant, it was always Vernon Rudolph who made it tick. His key employees, whom Vernon recruited with the greatest of patience and care, were fearful of him, scornful of his weaknesses, and yet absolutely loyal to him. Vernon's lifeblood was his business. He did not have much of a personal life, since he lived and breathed Krispy Kreme.

Here are his secrets:

1. He knew his business. He ran that first shop himself in 1937 with the crudest of equipment. No one could pull the wool over his eyes, because he knew how to run a doughnut shop.

2. He had a fantastic ability to think and plan ahead. He would think big, think leverage, and he did not make mistakes. In one doughnut shop he saw the start of something big, and he had the unique ability to multiply it. I think Vernon would have been extraordinarily successful in any business he tackled; doughnuts just happened to be the game he chose.

3. Vernon never deviated into other fields. He knew doughnuts and he stuck to them in a fanatical way. It was years before he even agreed to sell soft drinks in his shops. His ultimate scorn was to see a pinball machine in a competitor's shop. After his death, Krispy Kreme was sold to a conglomerate. A few years later I was in Atlanta, Georgia, and stopped into a Krispy Kreme store. I found they were selling sandwiches along with their doughnuts. My only thought was that in heaven Vernon must be known as "Pinwheel Rudolph," because surely he was spinning in his grave.

4. Vernon was an expert in accomplishing vertical business integration. He dominated his industry, starting with the manufacture of the mixes, the design and manufacture of production equipment, retail stores, wholesale stores, private labeling, sale of ingredients, the entire spectrum of his industry.

5. "Eccentric" means "out of balance." Vernon was a hard worker to a fault. He was the personification of the work ethic.

6. He was a financial wizard, especially at achieving

leverage without making mistakes. He established an outstanding growth and profit record, and was charismatic in dealing with financial institutions. He was able to grow at his own pace, with financial help from the most prestigious banks and insurance companies. Vernon Rudolph was an extraordinary man whose approach was ethical, eccentric, and faultless in planning.

Now for another success story:

A father had two sons. The three of them operated a busy butcher shop. Their meats were so good that customers waiting in line scarcely asked the price. I was engaged to Peggy Fitzpatrick and had invited her to dinner. I stopped in their shop and asked for two really good steaks. The butcher brought out what appeared to be a whole side of beef and began to dissect it. About fifteen minutes later, he had extracted two steaks from the very core. The rest was all over his cutting block. The steaks, of course, were superb. I became a regular customer of this family business because it was always a pleasant experience to shop there. The owners were happy and their customers were happy. They were business winners, like Vernon Rudolph, but in a different way. And I suspect they enjoyed their business every bit as much as Vernon did. They surely had more leisure time.

My old friend Frank Milne, who owns the Chevrolet agency specializing in Corvettes, has always been a successful businessman. Before becoming the owner, he worked at the agency for twenty years, first as sales manager, and then for many years as general manager. The owners of the business finally wanted to retire and sold the agency to Frank. Frank is the kind of person who is good at what he does, and happy doing it.

The source of his success is his love of the business. He is devoted to cars, and has always been proud of his products and services. Love of the business, coupled with managerial experience and ability, has made him a natural success. If you are really attached to some field, don't give it up unless it is completely impractical as a business.

LEARN FROM OTHERS 145

Now for some poor businessmen. The first example is a fellow we will call Pete. He is a fine man: honest, hardworking, kind, and intelligent. He has undertaken a number of businesses over a period of years, and every one has resulted in disaster. Pete is the classic example of a guy who, in spite of Herculean effort, just can't win. In contrast, I am sure you know people who seem to have some special knack with making a business work, and do it with ease and style. You may have wondered just what makes the difference between the perennial loser and the one who wins with ease. Perhaps this story will give you some pointers.

I have given a good deal of thought to identifying the reasons for Pete's failures. He was always in too much of a hurry. At one time he decided to take up jogging. He had great enthusiasm, but he was unwilling to approach the sport with the necessary start-up training. I cautioned him to take it easy. His irrepressible urge was to run too far, too fast, too soon. He was defeated before he started. He simply burned out by overtaxing himself. In looking at all of his business undertakings, I detected the same characteristic. His was an attitude of urgency and speed rather than one of prudence and pace. He always burned himself out, just as he did in his jogging program.

Pete had other traits that also worked against his success. In every business he started, he sold his product too cheaply. His approach was to set a price that would be lower than anybody else in town. As a result of his emphasis on low price, he focused his attention on how cheaply the product could be produced. This meant that the quality of his products suffered and they were rejected by his customers.

Pete was always optimistic to the point of being euphoric. He was an outstanding salesman and pleasant in all situations. His enthusiasm and selling ability, however, tended to get in the way of calculating risks carefully. He was not a cautious person but plunged ahead, fueling his momentum with enthusiasm.

There was still another reason for Pete's failures. He was not able to learn from his mistakes. Time after time he would plunge pell-mell into a new business, never stopping to identify mistakes from the previous attempts. He made the same mistakes again. Pete went too fast, sold too cheaply, did not focus on product quality, and did not calculate risk.

Another loser was a Cuban fellow whom I will call José. José bought a going business that had been operating successfully as a Mexican restaurant. When José took over, he made an assumption that proved to be a serious mistake. He assumed everyone felt as he did about Cuban food, which he dearly loved. He changed the menu from Mexican dishes to Cuban dishes and found that the sales gradually dropped to a disastrous level.

Start-up business people do not have the luxury of indulging in idiosyncrasies. Ride the horse in the direction the horse is going. If you want to test your preferences, then by all means test them; but do not bet all your money on the outcome. José could have taken over the restaurant and not lost a dollar of sales by simply operating it as before. If he did a better job at what was already accepted, he would have increased his sales. At the same time he could have tested a single Cuban delicacy and found out fast enough what the response would be, without risking and losing the entire business.

Another loser is a fellow we will call Ed. Ed was about fifty-five years old and had been in the pizza business for years. He was operating in a shopping center when we opened a new doughnut shop in the same center. Shortly after we opened, Ed came into our new shop to see me. He was completely dejected. He asked if we could teach him to make doughnuts, because his pizza business was ready to fold.

Ed finally disclosed his problem. He was unable to sell beer and wine, and without these items he had lost almost all of his dining room business. His story was dismal. The shopping center had a beer bar with a clause in its lease prohibiting any other tenant from selling beer or wine. Ed was advised of this restriction by the landlord before he signed his lease.

He signed the lease anyway. He could not imagine his pizza business conflicting with the beer bar, and assumed the bar operator would not object to his selling beer and wine. Proceeding on this assumption, he spent $3500 for fixtures and interior decoration. When Ed went to the beer bar owner for clearance to sell beer, he was turned down. The bar operator felt that beer sold in the pizza shop would reduce his own sales. Ed opened without beer and soon found himself drowning.

A person who expects to achieve success in business must exercise a reasonable degree of prudence. When Ed first considered the location he could have avoided endless grief by asking, "Would you mind if I sell beer and wine in my pizza restaurant?" He would have either received approval or passed on to another location. Exercise caution in your business as you would for your personal safety. If you wander onto a freeway you might be hit by a bus. Don't be hit like the pizza man.

Here is the story of a bright young man I will call Dave. He graduated from college with great self-assurance. He left a job to take over his father's business, which was encountering serious difficulties. Dave's father operated a food-vending business and Dave was successful in turning it around and enlarging it into a profitable operation. To handle their growing business, Dave rented a huge but run-down building in the center of town. The rent was low and there was more space than they needed at the time.

The taste of success encouraged Dave to broaden into other businesses. The first step was to convert the front of this huge building into a dinner-house restaurant. It was beautifully done and became the talk of the town. Above and around the dining room of the restaurant was an enormous mezzanine, and this became a discotheque.

In another part of the building was an unused store front that Dave rebuilt into a theater in the round. Part of the old building had previously been operated as a flea-bag hotel, and this was repainted and upgraded into a somewhat better apartment hotel.

Unfortunately Dave could not possibly control all these operations, so ultimately each of the businesses began to deteriorate. Finally everything was sold to satisfy the creditors. Dave was left with a clean slate from which to start again.

After the failure, Dave had a foundation made up of finely crushed dreams on which to build a new future. Crushed dreams make a good foundation provided they are mixed with the proper understanding of what went wrong. In Dave's case, he diversified into businesses in which he had no experience. Also, he tried to run a number of unfamiliar businesses all at the same time. Surely he had learned the value of moderating confidence with caution.

These case histories of good and bad businessmen can be put to good use by the start-up entrepreneur. From the good businessmen, sort out winning techniques and go do the same. We all emulate those we admire. You probably know people you have admired so much you found yourself picking up their phrases of speech. Why not then emulate business people who have succeeded? Pick up on their style and how they go about business.

Other business people who have not done well have made mistakes, and we all can learn from them. People who failed in business did so because their mode of operation didn't work. From the losers you can learn what made them fail, and then avoid it!

These case histories reveal the following composite picture of a good business person and a bad one. They are listed side by side to provide a visual image of the differences between the two.

The people who are winners seem to be experienced, specialized, cautious, quality-minded, and happy. The losers are always the plungers who are inexperienced in what they begin.

Come up with your own list of good and bad traits by making up a list of a half dozen business people you have known. Review each of their histories and write down their traits. Then make up your own composite list of the traits of the winners and another of the losers. This can be a valuable game for the start-up entrepreneur to play. Learn from the experience of others.

THE GOOD AND THE BAD BUSINESS PERSON

Good	Bad
1. Has clear-cut goals.	1. Impetuous.
2. Pays attention to details.	2. Sense of urgency.
3. Attracts and keeps good employees.	3. Feels need to grow fast.
4. Sells value instead of cheap price.	4. Euphoric optimism.
5. Works hard.	5. Lacks focus on quality.
6. Cool and cautious.	6. Does not learn from mistakes.
7. Is ethical.	7. Personal preference emphasized.
8. Delegates well.	8. Bets everything on high risk.
9. Some are eccentric (all work).	9. Does not test first.
10. Knows business by experience.	10. Not prudent in big decisions.
11. Plans ahead.	11. Overconfident.
12. Sticks with one business.	12. Starts without experience.
13. Expands by vertical integration.	13. Runs more than one business.
14. Has financial acumen.	14. Diversified, not specialized.
15. Calculates risks carefully.	15. Unhappy with work.
16. Quality without compromise.	16. Sometimes flamboyant.
17. Service without compromise.	
18. Very good at what he does.	
19. Experienced before starting.	
20. Loves his product.	
21. Loves his work.	
22. Unhurried in accomplishing goals.	

21

HORROR STORY

When you are preparing to go into business, there are two things to learn: what to do and what not to do. This is a what-not-to-do chapter, the story of how I went broke. The company I started and operated for ten years went bankrupt. After years of doing well, I found myself at the bottom of a private hell that I had created myself. I was forty-four years old. I share the story with you so you will benefit from my experience. It was a bad time of my life during which terror and shame were my companions, but over a period of years the harsh memory has diminished. As a lawyer remarked at the time, going broke is like a sickness; in time you get over it.

The key issues I wish to convey are the fatal defects in judgment that resulted in the disaster. By sharing this hindsight view of my own experience in failure, you may find some rules that can be of use in your own business.

Up to the point where I made a few disastrous decisions, I had enjoyed success in business. I was the fellow who in thought, word, and deed was good at business and always a winner. My years of doing well blinded me into overlooking some signposts that would have been obvious to a more prudent person. Judgment can be dulled by success or terribly handicapped by inexperience.

I had been a general contractor for a number of years and had my own firm, which specialized in "total responsibility" construction. The firm carried out all aspects of development for clients, including architecture, financing, construction, and property management, on a contract basis. Over a period of ten years my company built at least 150 projects, primarily small apartment buildings.

In the Los Angeles area, around 1968, a surplus of apartments was built. At the same time, financing for projects dried up. This left my company with a drastically reduced volume of business. During this period, while apartment construction was coming to a standstill, another business was beginning to grow rapidly—franchising. One of the most popular areas for franchising was that of food operations. In most cases the operators featured specialized menus, coupled with uniquely designed, single-purpose buildings.

One of the greatest problems for many of the food franchisers was real estate: that is, the design, financing, and construction of the units themselves. My firm was well qualified in real estate development, and this ability, coupled with the sudden and drastic drop in our apartment backlog, led me to start a franchised restaurant operation as a subsidiary of the construction firm. I then merged the franchising operations and the construction businesses into one entity.

I won't bore you or flog myself with the details, but the food operations were ultimately unsuccessful. We performed well in the areas in which my construction company had experience: architecture and construction. The operating restaurants, however, were not successful and the final result was total disaster.

I learned a number of lessons from this horror story. Read them carefully, for they are the distillation of too many sleepless nights and later, careful contemplation of what went wrong.

Lesson Number One: Never, never get involved in a business in which the following two elements are both present at the same time: 1. The business is a high risk. 2. All of your savings are at stake.

There are times to take high risks and there are times to bet all of your chips. Never do both at the same time. The best example of this is the game of Russian roulette: it's high risk with everything at stake. It is easy for us to see the folly of Russian roulette, but you would be surprised how many play this same game when going into business.

In my own case, high risk was present because I was entering into a business (restaurants) in which I had no experience.

However, it is not necessary to commit all of your assets to test a high-risk undertaking. I could have tested this undertaking without committing my successful construction business. But risking everything I had in this new venture was just like picking up that Russian roulette revolver and pulling the trigger.

There are times when you might want to take high risks; just be sure you are careful to spot them as such. Here are some examples:

1. Starting a new business.
2. Lack of experience in the business.
3. Partnerships.
4. Lack of experience in business management.
5. Expanding an operating business rapidly.
6. Expanding into new geographic areas.

Whenever you do go into a high-risk situation, limit your exposure to no more than a predetermined amount. For example, if you have $30,000 in savings and wish to start a business, then perhaps you should expose only $10,000 to loss. In such a case, do not sign a long-term lease on a location, but insist on a short-term one with options to extend. You surely should not give any personal guarantees that exceed the $10,000.

Thus, when you go into high risks, do so in a very calculated way. Like taking a fling at the craps tables in Las Vegas, decide before you leave just how much you are willing to lose and take only that amount along.

Our purpose of this book is to show you how to take the craps-shoot out of going into business. You can't eliminate the risk at Las Vegas, but you surely can when you become an entrepreneur. The worst high risk is to go into business without having first experienced it by working for someone else. You eliminate the risk by learning the business before starting.

There are other times you may wish to commit all of your resources to a business. The time to commit everything is when you are sure of the outcome. The time to sign those leases and personal guarantees is when you are experienced and have a business that works.

Lesson Number Two: If you are good at your business, like it, and are successful at it, then stick with it through the thick and thin of the inevitable cycles of business prosperity and recession. Learn how to operate profitably in periods of prosperity. Learn to pull in your horns during recessions, and to retrench and endure the adverse swings of the business pendulum. There is a separate chapter devoted to this subject, Chapter 30, "Shoemaker, Stick to Thy Last."

Lesson Number Three: Put your toe in the water first before you plunge in. Become personally experienced in the very heart of the business before you commit to it. Prove, before you execute plans. You would not jump into 100 feet of water if you did not know how to swim. Don't jump into a business unless you have proved it by experiencing it.

In setting out for yourself, there won't be anyone along who will tap you on the shoulder and say, "Hey, Joe, you have just taken a wrong turn for reasons A, B, and C." There were many knowledgeable and intelligent people around when I made my incredible mistakes leading to failure. There were CPAs, franchising experts, food experts, legal experts, and design experts. Not one of them knew the basic pitfalls I have just described to you. This kind of failure clears away the conceptual fog and reveals the real do's and don'ts to a prospective entrepreneur. For you, this book can be the tap on the shoulder when you need it.

I will close this chapter with one observation about going broke. Aside from the shame, it is like being left alone on a desert island. You may have heard the cynical expression "A friend in need is a friend to avoid." This will be the attitude of ninety-five out of a hundred of your friends. But let me tell you: the ninety-five were not really friends at all. The others are your friends, and you will be able to count them on one hand. And you will learn the meaning of having true friends. Bless you all: Bob, Chuck, Jim, and my dear friend in heaven, Lenny.

22
HIT THE BEACHES

The greatest risk you will ever take in business is the act of starting. When you execute the plan, you're not playing games anymore: this is for real. Real money. Real risks. If you fail, real shame. If you win, real rewards.

Getting started in business is like gaining a beachhead in war. It will be your Operation Overlord and the whole attempt will be at stake, as it was for Eisenhower at Normandy. If you fail to establish your beachhead, your future is uncertain and your new business could be doomed.

Some military experts gave Eisenhower only a fifty-fifty chance of success. Bad weather could have created havoc. Better German intelligence could have pinpointed resistance and driven him back into the sea. To succeed in Operation Overlord, Eisenhower needed everything going for him. It took incredible preparation, know-how, and courage to win that beachhead. It took every man and every gun that could be mustered by all of the Allied forces. The highest risks were at the outset, when the signal was finally given to hit the beaches.

The greatest single deterrent to starting a business is the fear of failure. If this were not so, many more people would indeed be in business for themselves, because the benefits are so good. As in war, the highest risks occur when you actually start. Risk diminishes as the business matures. Mature companies that experience failure are not at all common: the casualties occur when the business starts up.

Once you have secured your business beachhead, you can penetrate and consolidate and the do-or-die risk becomes history. Let's use the Normandy invasion of Europe as our guideline. Put yourself in the role of Eisenhower, the supreme commander. What were the keys to his success? When you think about it you see that he had everything in readiness first. The planning, the power, and the know-how were all mustered together and completely ready before the attack.

Your approach to starting a business must be the same as Eisenhower's tactics in hitting the beaches. Go in with every gun loaded. Your forces are the chapter headings you have read under Step Three of this book, "Planning the Attack."

Step One, "Do I Want To Be in Business?" should again be verified. Stop and review Chapter 6, which provides a format for answering this question. Step Two provides a means for deciding which business to begin. Then, if you still have the desire to be in your own business and you have chosen one, you can proceed to the plan of attack. Review each of the forces to be used in your business start-up. Here they are:

"PLANNING THE ATTACK" CHECKLIST

Chapter	Needed Before Starting	Score 1-10 on your state of readiness
12 Partners	I can objectively evaluate a partnership.	_____
13 Learn by Doing	I have worked for someone else in the same business.	_____
14 Quality Without Compromise	QWC is included in my plans.	_____
15 Pilot Operation First	I will test first with a pilot operation.	_____
16 H.B.S., I Love You	I have taken business management courses.	_____
17 Shall I Franchise?	No, but I may learn from one.	_____
18 Keep Score	I have completed accounting courses and will initially keep my own books.	_____

Chapter	Needed Before Starting	Score 1-10 on your state of readiness
19 Cash Flow	I have used cash control to determine capital required and will use it to control liquidity.	
20 Learn from Others	I will emulate traits of successful entrepreneurs and avoid those of losers.	
21 Horror Story	I will not risk all my resources on starting a business.	

Don't hesitate to dramatize your start-up as I have done here. Take this quite seriously, because the consequences of failure can be lots of unhappiness. In your business beachhead you don't have a lot of blood to give. Never start up with piecemeal preparation. Have everything in readiness.

Now, what if the worst thing happens: you start up and fail? If you're a real entrepreneur, you go back to square one and start up all over again. This time you will have the benefit of your experiences. I tell you with all my heart that business too can be sweeter the second time around.

In summary, have everything going for you initially. This includes the support of your family. Start small, in control, and build from earnings. Don't go against the facts or against your instinct. Compare and evaluate. Use the "Planning the Attack" checklist.

STEP FOUR

OPERATIONS

This section on operations goes into the action of starting a business. You have made your decision to start and have completed all of the preparatory steps. Now I will give you suggestions on operating your business that you won't find in the classroom.

23

LOCATION, LOCATION, LOCATION

Your first step to get a business into operation is to decide on where to locate it, not unlike Eisenhower choosing Normandy. Your selection of your first location will have an overwhelming impact on your chances for success. It is the old classic question, "What are the three most important parts of a piece of real estate?" The title of this chapter answers the question. The first two chapters in "Operations" will deal with your first location: how to choose it and how to negotiate a lease for it.

Some months ago I met a lady who was about to open a cookie shop. The location was a sidewalk storefront on Ventura Boulevard in Studio City, California. I knew that she was doomed before she even started. That location had three fatal flaws for a cookie shop: 1. It had no off-street parking. 2. It had no foot traffic. 3. There were no other customer-generators nearby.

I stopped by to see how she was setting up her new shop. She was doing everything just right. She had the right equipment, the right plan (cookies only), cute decor, quality ingredients. She had everything it took to be successful, with one exception—the location. She had put her savings into fixtures and new equipment, and spent weeks of hard work getting ready to open. Heaven knows what debt and rent obligations she had undertaken. Yet she was defeated, without even being aware of it, because of the location. Six months later she went out of business.

If anyone needs a good location, it is the person just starting up. But the start-up person is the one least likely to know the criteria for a good location, or have the know-how to make a deal for it. As a business matures, the do's and don'ts regarding locations become apparent, because you gain from experience. So your first location becomes a very important decision and you must approach it with all of the knowledge you can bring to bear.

In deciding on a location, you will be competing with large companies that are stronger than you. These competitors already know the do's and don'ts and even if they do make a mistake they have an established chain that can support their losers.

Large, mature chains develop sophisticated "site models" in order to evaluate new locations. Computers are used to analyze criteria and determine potential sales. Decisions are therefore based on facts, not subjective opinions.

The selection of your first location is a decision that can mean success or failure. In the retail doughnut business we experience significant variation in sales from one location to another. Some new stores produce sales higher than expected; others can be a disappointment, and all because of location.

I must confess that we are not much concerned with most competitors who operate single doughnut shops, because their judgment about location is usually bad anyway. Many independent competitors pick their locations for all of the wrong reasons. Let's go over the pitfalls to become aware of how mistakes are made. Later we will go over some positive rules.

The first pitfall is to judge a site on the basis of rent. Cheap rent is appealing, and high rent is forbidding. Rent is important, but it must be evaluated separately from location, as we will do later in the chapter.

Second pitfall: pick a site based on a hunch or impulse. You see it; you like it; you take it. The word "criterion" is not in your vocabulary. According to Webster's "criterion" means "A standard of judging; a rule or test by which anything is tried in forming a correct judgment respecting it."

Also, you are itchy to get started and have a sense of urgency in picking a location. Force yourself to be slow and deliberate. There is no such thing as the last good site. There will always be endless opportunities for good locations.

Another pitfall in picking a location is to leave the decisions to others, such as your real estate broker or the shopping center developer.

And finally, to put the finishing touches on a poor location, let the lessor work out the terms of the lease for you. What is best for the lessor is probably not in your best interest.

Knowing what not to do can be as valuable as having accurate criteria of what locations are best for your business. Now for the positive approach in selecting your first location.

First, learn the best location criteria for your business by determining those used by the most successful of your competitors. Make a detailed analysis, then use their criteria as your own. If the lady opening the cookie shop had done this, she would have realized that cookie shops have been successful in enclosed malls, or where there is an extremely high density of foot traffic and impulse buyers.

Here are the criteria for our chain of retail doughnut shops:

1. Traffic count. (Available by a phone call to the city public works department.) We want 25,000 cars per day.
2. Traffic speed. The slower the better.
3. Proximity to the sidewalk. Our sales occur early in the morning, when customers do not go into an enclosed shopping center.
4. Visibility. A function of signs.
5. Access. On-site parking that is easy.
6. Proximity of competition. (An adverse factor.)
7. Income level of neighborhood. Medium to low is best for us.

8. Population density.

9. Proximity to specific customer generators. These include shopping centers and work-destination centers.

10. Adverse factors: Being near a high school creates problems for us. Learn the adverse factors that contribute to a poor location for your own business.

11. Being on the "going to work" side of the street.

12. Age factor of neighborhood. We look for young families with children, who are the most frequent doughnut eaters.

How did we develop these criteria? Before our first store opened we learned from other competitors who ran successful stores. After we got started, each of our own new stores added to our know-how.

Keep in mind that each and every business has its own specialized criteria. For example, we want to be on the side of the street people use to drive to work because doughnuts and coffee are eaten in the morning. On the other hand, a liquor store will surely want the opposite side of the street, which is used by people going home from work. A cookie shop will thrive in an enclosed mall, but a doughnut shop would be risky there because of the absence of early morning business. So you must determine your own specialized criteria and not use those appropriate to another business. Every business has absolutely unique criteria, like fingerprints, and you must learn the exact fingerprint that applies to yours.

Let's assume you have your criteria in hand. There is a word you should now handle with ease: "No." Learn to say *no* when a site doesn't meet your criteria. I assure you the world is full of sites that will. As my old friend Vernon Rudolph used to say, you just have to keep turning over rocks to find the worms. Patiently seek out the site that conforms to your criteria.

One factor that is important to our business might also be important to you: the proximity and density of competition. There are lots of ponds to fish in, and our experience is that we do better when we fish in a pond that is not so crowded. In our business, it does not make good sense to open next to a strong competitor. Inevitably, the competing stores will divide the sales, resulting in two mediocre operations. Furthermore, you are not going to dislodge a large, strong competitor who has holding power. Rather, you will run the risk of being smothered yourself.

Take time in picking your first location. Don't rush your decision. Remember, there is no such thing as the last good site. Spend time on location work by driving on surface streets (not freeways). The more time you spend in your car looking, the more you will be exposed to good locations.

When you find a location that is a real beauty, you will know it from the first glance and have great enthusiasm for it. The enthusiasm comes from the site's clear-cut conformity to your criteria. Before opening the first Yum Yum Shop, I spent a great amount of time learning the best criteria. The first store had to be successful because it was going to be my start. Then I looked and looked and looked. When I saw that first location on North Figueroa Street in Los Angeles, there was no question that it was what I wanted. It was the end store in a shopping center, where a prior food tenant had gone broke. It was a low-income neighborhood.

Other tenants in the center thought that it was silly for me to sell only doughnuts, but they didn't know the criteria for a doughnut shop. Now, years later, Yum Yum number one is still there and is paying more than triple the fixed rent due to what the landlord receives in percentage overage. My enthusiasm for that first site was based on its conformity to criteria that had a bearing on only one business: a doughnut shop and nothing else. When you learn your own criteria, you will also get the same sense of excitement when you spot a great location.

Conversely, there will be other locations you will discover or will have suggested to you that will leave you undecided. You will find yourself asking others for their opinions, in order to kick yourself off the dead center of indecision. I have gone through this experience many times, and in instances in which I have decided to "go," the results were usually disappointing.

Unless you find that a site is absolutely right and demonstrates exciting conformity with your criteria, the best decision is to say no. Pass the dice to someone else. Never find yourself needing to be convinced that a location is OK: just say no. There are too many problems with low-volume stores, and too many opportunities for superstores.

Here is a simple checklist to use in selecting your first and future locations. You must answer the following three questions affirmatively if a location is right for you.

First: Is the location in an area where you want to be? This question can have both personal and business implications. From the personal standpoint, it is important to be where you really want to be. If you like Laguna Beach and would love to live there, shouldn't this have consideration? From the business standpoint also, the area must certainly be considered. No matter what business you are in, there are some areas that are better than others, so you might as well be in the best. You will never see a Yum Yum Donut Shop in Sun City, California, a retirement community in the desert. It is hot, it has a very high average age, and is therefore not a good area for our business.

Second: Is the location the best available in the area? This question assumes you have already selected the area, and now you are picking the location. "Best available" is the key phrase, and may mean the location is not the very best. I would love to see one of our stores on the key, central intersection of town. The problem is usually that it's just not available. Or the best location may not make sense from the standpoint of rental cost. Some businesses can pay more rent than you can, so they preempt certain locations where you would like to be. To determine which site is the best available means you have complete knowledge of alternative locations. Do not decide until you are familiar with all other possibilities. Then when you do decide, you can be confident you have selected the best one available.

Third: Does the location meet your criteria? You have selected your area and determined the best available location in it. Now, apply your final yardstick, your criteria. You should have developed them in detail by now, and should include a checklist that applies to your business.

A final consideration is how much rent can you afford to pay. It has been our experience that better located and therefore higher-rent stores have been more profitable due to resulting higher sales. We gradually worked up to this conclusion through experience. As a start-up, you will not have the sales experience on which to base your ability to pay rent. You will probably start on a lower rent basis because your sales forecast will (at least, one hopes) be conservative.

In our business we can pay 9 percent of our sales in rent. Let us assume we have a potential location that we estimate will do $5000 per week in sales. This means we can afford $5000 × 9 percent, or $450 per week in rent. Convert this to a monthly figure by multiplying by the number of weeks in a month (4.3), and arrive at $1935 per month. This is the amount of rent we could afford if sales are $5000 per week. Therefore it would not profit us to pay $3000 per month for a store in which we project only $5000 in sales per week.

Select the very best location you can afford. You should not go into business with the crippling handicap of a poor location; your first must be the best.

Now, with your carefully selected location in mind and an anticipated rent that you can afford, let's go into negotiating the lease.

24
YOUR FIRST LEASE

The following guidelines can be used for all three types of business space: commercial, office, or industrial. You will be dealing with tough, experienced landlords whose primary goal is to extract the highest rent possible from unsophisticated tenants.

Commercial properties are sold to real estate investors primarily on the basis of the return that the properties produce. While the return varies depending on the type and quality of project, let us say that 10 percent is the going rate on the property in which you want to lease space.

The value of the property, since it is based on return, becomes a function of how much rent you, the tenant, are willing to pay. This creates a highly leveraged reason for the landlord to negotiate a high rent. For example, let's assume you wish to rent 1000 square feet of space and the fair, going rental is $1000 per month. If the landlord can convince you to pay $1300, he has achieved a great deal more than $300 per month in additional rent. He has added $36,000 to his profit when the building is sold.

While this sounds farfetched, keep in mind that $300 per month times 12 produces $3600 in additional annual income, which, capitalized at 10 percent, adds $36,000 to the price of the project. What keeps the landlord from getting more than he should? There are a number of restraints.

First, the going rents created by supply and demand in the marketplace will limit what a landlord can charge. The prudence of the prospective tenant will also, one hopes, moderate what rent is acceptable. The tenant's ability to negotiate and his knowledge of lease terms have a bearing on how much rent is paid. Finally, older properties that have vacancies will, to a varying degree, control the rentals that are charged on newer space.

Signing a lease could be the largest obligation you will undertake in starting a business. It can be enormous. If you lease a space for $1000 per month for five years, come rain or shine you are obligated to pay $1000 × 12 months × 5 years, or $60,000.

Before getting into a checklist of leasing issues to be careful about, there are two overriding safeguards that are essential. They will be a very strong sword to protect you. First, have a competent lawyer to represent you. His presence is just as important as in any other start-up activity. Your lawyer's value is not in constructing nit-picking phraseology but in protecting you on the important issues. There is an old phrase to keep in mind when negotiating the lease: "Don't count the ants while the elephants march by."

The second edge of your protective sword is that you do not sign a long-term lease for your first location. You may feel that to tie up a location for a long time requires a long-term lease, but your first store will be a high risk by virtue of your inexperience.

There is a way out of this dilemma that landlords appreciate as the prudent answer for the start-up entrepreneur. Have a short-term lease (say one year) with a number of short-term renewable options that cover a long period of time. Thus you can escape from a poor location after one year, but if it is good and you are successful, you will have it tied up. Once you have gained momentum in your business and are adding new locations, it won't be necessary to hedge by signing short-term leases with options.

Now, with the double-edge sword of having a lawyer and not signing a long lease, let's review a checklist of important lease issues. While some items apply only to retail space, others apply to all business locations. There will probably be other items you and your lawyer will want to check.

Percentage Rent. This is a standard clause in most shopping center leases. We pay a 5 percent overage rent in order to secure locations we want. If the store is a good one, we will pay the overage and be very happy to do so. A low-profit-margin business such as a grocery store could not afford 5 percent overage, so this figure will vary with the nature of the business.

Cost-of-Living Clause. With the prospects of hyperinflation, this is a dynamite issue. Most leases prepared by landlords include a cost-of-living clause which provides that the rent escalate each year with the cost-of-living index. Never agree to a landlord's cost-of-living clause. Go along with a modified form in order to secure top locations. A landlord will argue that if the cost of living goes up, it would be normal to expect that selling prices would go up accordingly. Neither he nor you, however, could control a runaway inflation, and you surely cannot assume that your pricing can keep pace with inflation. Agree to cost-of-living adjustments made only in five-year periods, and not on an annual basis. Also, insist that the adjustment not exceed 4 percent per year. This limitation of 4 percent per year will be helpful over the long pull, assuming that actual cost-of-living increases exceed this amount. Landlords normally go along with a modified cost-of-living clause.

Signs. A lease normally provides that you can have signs so long as the landlord approves them. Prepare dimensioned drawings of all signs, and make this a part of the lease. The signs should be the maximum size permitted by the local sign ordinance. If you execute a lease without specific agreement on signs, your landlord will be difficult to deal with later. He will be more agreeable and anxious to accommodate you before the lease is signed. Local sign companies are willing to check the local codes and prepare drawings without requiring you to sign a contract with them.

Contingencies. Put contingencies in your lease. Anything the landlord represents or agrees to but is not in the lease should be included as a contingency. If a landlord refuses to make a lease contingent on something he has promised, assume you will not get it. It's best to deal with someone who will spell out what he has promised.

Subletting. You should have the right to sublet the premises for other uses. If your business does not work out, you will want to put someone else in. It is not unfair for the landlord to include the phrase: "Subject to the approval of the landlord, which approval shall not be unreasonably withheld." The expression "not be unreasonably withheld" is vital to have in the lease. If this is not spelled out, the landlord can refuse to approve any subtenant.

Parking Rights. Have your parking rights in the lease. This can be handled by an exhibit (drawing) showing the parking spaces you have a right to.

Leasehold Improvements. Have a clearly defined plan and specifications as to the leasehold improvements the landlord is expected to make for you. Make this a part of the lease document. Your lawyer will show you how.

Personal Guarantees. Many landlords will ask for your personal guarantee, and I recommend that you not give one. If it becomes a make-or-break point and you feel the location is critical to your success, there are certain limitations your personal guarantee should include:

1. The guarantee should never exceed your total obligation for rent. If the landlord's cost is less than the total rent obligation, your guarantee should extend only to these costs. For example, if your building costs $50,000 (excluding land), and your total rent is $100,000, then you should guarantee only what the landlord has spent, $50,000. The landlord's improvement costs should be spelled out in the guarantee.

2. During each succeeding lease year, the extent of your guarantee should be a fraction of the improvement cost determined by the following:

$$\frac{\text{Remaining years of lease}}{\text{Total years of lease}}$$

In this way, your guarantee diminishes as the lease matures.

3. The personal guarantee should be released when you reach a stipulated net worth, or when your obligations are assumed by another party whose net worth is a stipulated amount.

The form of your personal guarantee is a job for your attorney. Since the landlord's primary interest is renting vacant space, you will generally find he will be amenable to a limited personal guarantee.

Landlord's Approvals. Whenever the lease calls for the landlord's approval, have it also state that the landlord will not unreasonably withhold his approval. The items in a lease that require landlord approval should be limited to future events, such as subletting. All conditions going into the lease should be spelled out.

Reciprocal Remedies. A landlord's lease might maintain that in the event of a dispute, the tenant is to pay for legal expenses incurred by the landlord. A reciprocal remedy would say that the prevailing party shall be reimbursed for legal expenses. Reciprocal remedies should be inserted throughout the lease, wherever appropriate.

Special Requirements of Tenant. When we negotiate a lease for a doughnut shop, we insert a sentence stating that the landlord approves our installing newspaper stands outside the shop. Customers buying coffee and doughnuts in the morning like to buy newspapers. While the lease is being negotiated, the landlords don't object to this relatively small point because they want the lease signed. A later request for approval usually meets with a negative attitude, such as "Newsstands are ugly and we don't want them in our shopping center." You may have special items of your own to be covered by the lease. Any specialized requirements that are important to you should be made a part of your own checklist.

Exhibits. Your lease may require exhibits: for example, a drawing of the plan to show the available parking. This exhibit might not be important now, but later it could prevent the possibility of the landlord's replacing parking in front of your store with another building. Another exhibit might outline your space in red, to prevent any possible misunderstanding of where you are located.

Time Limit for Acceptance. When you make an offer to rent space, the landlord should either accept it, continue to negotiate, or reject it. To avoid his doing nothing at all or shopping it around, include a sentence that makes your offer subject to the landlord's approval within thirty (or fewer) days.

Leasehold Improvements. The reason to rent space is that it ties up too much money to own it. Be wary of investing dollars in tenant improvements. Your cash can be used more effectively in business operations. Often, changes or improvements are necessary in the building. These become part of the building and are called "leasehold improvements." Have the lessor provide these improvements for you, and have the rent include a fair return on how much the improvements cost. Therefore, to arrive at how much total rent to pay, the costs of tenant improvements must be determined by a cost breakdown. Normally, the lessor will provide improvements according to agreed-upon plans, and also an agreed-upon additional rent to cover their costs.

The foregoing items can be used as a checklist of points not to be overlooked. Create your own additional list of issues that are important to you.

You will probably be asked to sign a form lease which has been prepared by the landlord. Form leases are prepared by lawyers who are paid to protect the landlord. A "landlord" lease can be so inequitable that even a beginner will feel a surge of indignation when reading it. You want a fair lease, and to achieve this you must be familiar with the process of making one—otherwise you will find yourself at a disadvantage.

A standard-form lease that has been prepared by a landlord can be modified and made equitable. I know, because we do it all the time. You must realize that only a relatively few aspects of a lease are of major importance. First, you decide the rent that makes sense. If what you can afford is less than what is asked, fill in the rent you can afford and strike out what the landlord has filled in. Then go through the entire lease item by item to be sure the significant elements are modified to conform to a reasonable agreement. Change every item that is important to you, and restate it in fair terms. For each change you make, put your initials in the margin. Then, resubmit the modified landlord's form with your signature. If the landlord accepts your modifications, he should also put his initials everywhere a change is made.

Your own checklist of lease items can be used in reviewing a landlord's lease form, so you do not overlook items that are important to you. Eliminate landlord contingencies, such as his approval of signs, and replace them with your own plans—your sign exhibit, for example. Include your own contingencies and specialized requirements, to customize the lease to your own needs. Remember, it is easier to get agreement on issues when the lease is negotiated; at a later stage it could be difficult or impossible.

When a landlord gets his own lease back, signed by you with changes made and initialed, he will know he is dealing with a reasonably prudent tenant. This may actually enhance your chances of making a deal with him. His alternative is to make a lopsided deal with a fool, who could cause him problems in the long haul. So to make a better lease and at the same time improve your chances of being considered, negotiate a lease that is reasonable for both parties. As long as you have the conditions that are important to you, don't object to the landlord's having his way in other items that are not important.

If your first store is in a large shopping center, you may not have leverage to require the landlord to completely customize the lease for you. If the center has, say, 500,000 square feet of rentable space, the landlord or his leasing agent may simply not agree to certain concessions and changes for your 1200 square feet. So it becomes a business judgment whether the strength of the location overrides the terms of a form lease. You may want to take a very desirable location even though the lease details are not completely ideal for your purposes.

You must keep a double perspective when negotiating your first lease. On one hand, you will be concerned with each detail of the lease. Details can come back later to give you grief, or provide an environment that will contribute to the success of your business.

On the other hand, the importance of major issues such as rent, length of lease, and cost-of-living terms will outweigh other issues. Once a fair lease is executed, you are free to concentrate on making your business work.

25
CREATE PROFIT CENTERS

Have you heard about how a thousand-mile journey starts? With the first step. Business success starts with a first step, too: the owner runs the store himself. Some never go beyond this first step. An entrepreneur who wishes to build a big company must break through the do-it-yourself operation.

The only way he can multiply his efforts is through other people. Therefore the key to a large business is managers. The key to managers is to create profit centers within your business and have managers motivated to operate these units in a way that makes money for you. Your success in transforming your start-up company into a large corporation will depend on your ability to create profit centers, and this chapter will show you how.

Before you apply the technique of profit centers, you should understand each operation by experiencing it. If you do not experience your manager's job, you must depend on your concept of it and your concept of how to operate a business and the reality of it could be totally different worlds. It would be difficult for you to create a successful profit-center plan without knowing how the center works.

My partner, Frank Watase, and I are both experienced in operating doughnut shops. We know how to make doughnuts, and we know all aspects of the day-to-day operations. We have experienced this by managing shops over a long enough period to have a real understanding of the business. With this experience, we are in a position to create the profit center. No manager is going to pull the wool over our eyes, because we've been there too. We know the key elements for proper control.

On the other hand, if we tried to design a profit center without knowing how the shop ticked, we could be ignoring fundamentals for success, and we might emphasize programs that are ineffectual. Without experience, we could create a profit center that simply did not work.

To prepare for turning an operation into a profit center, you should personally continue to operate it, and operate it profitably, until your company is financially strong enough to make the switch-over to the profit-center approach. Financial strength includes an adequate reserve of working capital to absorb the transition traumas. Finally, you should hang in there yourself until you are a professional at the game, and are completely comfortable and competent in operations.

With these qualifications under your belt, you are ready to convert your personally run business into a profit center. You are ready to create a structure in which your individual effort is multiplied by managers who will begin running your business for you.

There are only two ways you can motivate your profit-center managers: by reward and by recognition. Both are potent, and both should be used. Recognition alone is not enough. Sometimes reward without recognition works well, but the real answer is to employ both to motivate a manager.

We will deal primarily with reward motivation, and the reward will be limited to incentive pay, not ownership participation. Our approach, therefore, does not require you give up ownership interest in order to motivate your profit-center managers.

There are two keys to success in designing profit centers. The first is that it be a compartmentalized area of your business in which a manager can clearly exercise total responsibility and authority. For example, in our business a doughnut shop is a profit center. Our overall operations management of all the shops is a profit center. Our manufacturing and distribution business is a profit center. Our real estate operation is a profit center. Each of these profit centers could run as a separate business. Each is set up as a separate operation, run by a highly motivated manager.

The second key to a successful profit center is that the manager be on a plan in which his compensation relates to the success of his operation, that is, a profit-sharing arrangement. Reward then becomes the key incentive. It requires careful planning to custom-tailor the incentive to the profit center. The most successful reward motivation is achieved when a large percentage of a manager's total income comes from profit-sharing rather than salary. Roughly speaking, it is a matter of having at least 50 percent of total income from profit-sharing. The salary level should be somewhat less than the current rate offered for the management job.

Let's look at the profit-sharing part of the income. All profit-sharing plans use the financial income statement (profit and loss statement) as the measuring stick for how much bonus is paid. Each profit center has its own P&L. Profit-sharing can be set up on a leveraged or nonleveraged basis. We operate some of our profit centers on a leveraged basis (the doughnut shops) and others on a nonleveraged basis (top management centers). First I will explain the difference between these two approaches and then give you an example of each.

A leveraged profit-sharing plan is one in which the company's profit is extracted as an expense before arriving at the profit of the center. In this case the manager might receive all of the resulting bottom-line profit as his bonus. I refer to this as leveraged because the manager can do very well or very poorly. If the manager's center is profitable, the bonus will be good. On the other hand, the leverage created in this method can work negatively. If the center is only marginally profitable, the manager's bonus could be a negative number. In this instance, operating on a cumulative basis from one accounting period to the next, the manager could dig a deeper and deeper hole of minus profit-sharing on his P&L, and thus become discouraged.

A leveraged profit-sharing plan is the ultimate incentive for the manager to make a profit. Literally, a penny saved is a penny earned. Each penny he can produce in profit will result in a penny of bonus to him. Conversely, a penny wasted is a penny out of his pocket.

In a nonleveraged profit-sharing plan, the manager is paid a percentage of overall profits after actual expenses. Nonleveraged plans are more appropriate for larger-volume profit centers that are operated by the senior management of your company. In any plan, leveraged or nonleveraged, you will be setting up a profit-sharing system for an operation already in existence, one you have run yourself. Therefore you have a record of actual P&Ls that should be used to test your plan in advance. See what the results will be for your manager when you plug in your plan to the past P&Ls of the center. Will the manager be adequately motivated? Test the plan with the future in mind. Does it provide incentive for future layers of management?

Let's look at an example of a leveraged profit-sharing plan. For ease of numbers, assume the minimum salary for the manager is $250 per week. The motivation is created by a plan in which the manager receives 100 percent of the store's profit as bonus. The formula is simple: bonus = store profit. This is the ultimate form of leverage. Another element that makes this plan effective is that the profit is immediate. A weekly profit and loss statement means that the manager's bonus is paid weekly.

Each store's P&L includes expenses that give the company its necessary profit. The principal expense of this nature is a charge for overhead, which is a percentage of sales. Also, the store P&L is charged for accounting, supervision, and maintenance, all as a percentage of sales. In this manner the company expenses and profit are taken out of the store as expense items before the bottom-line profit is reached. The bottom-line profit becomes the bonus.

Let's look at an abbreviated weekly P&L of a leveraged profit-sharing plan for a profit center.

WEEKLY INCOME STATEMENT (P&L)

WEEK OF _____ THROUGH _____

Sales		3000
Purchases	1000	
Wages: Employees	550	
Manager's salary	250	
Rent	300	
Maintenance (2% of sales)	60	
Accounting (1% of sales)	30	
Supervision (2% of sales)	60	
Other expenses (itemized)	150	
Overhead expense (10% of sales)	300	
Total expenses	2700	2700
Net for the period		300
Bonus to be paid		300

In this example the manager has done well. He has made more in bonus ($300) than he made in salary ($250). His bonus essentially depends on elements within his own control, the first three items on the P&L: sales, purchases, and wages. If his employee wages had been $650 instead of $550, his bonus would have been reduced $100.

In this leveraged system, the manager has great control in determining the bonus he receives. If the manager's bonus is at least equal to his salary, it would be just about an optimum condition. That means the manager is earning twice what he would on salary. The powerful incentive, again, is that a penny saved is a penny earned and a penny wasted is a penny out of his pocket.

The essential requirement under this leveraged system is that the manager indeed makes some bonus income. When the manager does well, we know that a number of good things result. The company is satisfied because it has a profitable, trouble-free center operated by a successful manager. Also, the company can exercise supervisory control because the manager will maintain quality standards to protect his favorable income.

There are pros and cons to the leveraged system. The greatest advantage is a stable condition of control and profitability. Requiring the manager to conform to high standards will result in even higher sales, which result in a higher bonus, and the overall operation becomes an upward spiral.

On the other hand, there are potential problems with this leveraged system. Where the profit center is extraordinarily profitable, the company's profit is limited to a fixed percentage of sales, while the store profit (and therefore the manager's bonus) could become disproportionately large as a percentage of sales.

Another problem is that this system requires careful control to ensure that the manager does not become too frugal. The bonus is based on the manager's receiving all of the profit, which is calculated from sales and costs. You must be watchful that your manager does not create profit (and therefore bonus) by purchasing inferior merchandise, operating with too small a payroll to give adequate service, and all the endless other possibilities of improving profit at the expense of the future viability of the business.

Finally, a serious problem exists if your P&L for the center results in ongoing bottom-line losses rather than profits. To work, this system should be cumulative. A loss in one week must be made up before a subsequent week's profit is paid as bonus. If each week's P&L shows a loss, then the manager is simply digging a deeper and deeper hole of accumulated losses. When he wakes up and realizes that there is no way that losses can be made up, he will not only be nonmotivated, but he will also be negatively affected by the hole he is in.

It's clear that the P&L must show a profit for the leveraged system to work. While the tendency in a profitable center is to spend too little on wages and purchases (to create profit), the unprofitable center is likely to spend too much (because the manager has no incentive). So in a center whose P&L does not show a profit, it becomes important to institute adjustments to maintain incentive and control costs.

Now let's take a look at the nonleveraged incentive for operating a profit center. Again, the profit-sharing plan is based on the center's P&L. The greater the frequency in pulling P&Ls, the better will be the results. Also, frequent P&Ls will uncover problems earlier, so that small ones can be corrected before they grow.

A nonleveraged system gives the manager a percentage of the center's overall profit. Typically, it uses an actual P&L of the business. The manager's bonus is calculated before any provisions for corporate income tax. Let's look at a simple example on page 180. In this case, the manager's agreement is to receive a salary plus 10 percent of the center's profit.

The beauty of this system is that it benefits the owner if the manager makes a great deal of money in the form of profit-sharing. For every dollar the manager makes in profit-sharing, the owner will make nine dollars. When the business is growing, both the owner and the manager continue to share proportionately in the greater and greater rewards. No matter how great a sum the manager makes, there is still a good profit for the ownership. The key is never to change the deal, no matter how much the manager earns. A good manager is too valuable an asset to lose just because he is making too much money.

MONTHLY INCOME STATEMENT (P&L)

MONTH OF _____

Sales		300,000
Purchases	100,000	
Labor, including manager's salary	100,000	
All other actual costs	50,000	
Total costs	250,000	250,000
Profit before manager's profit sharing		50,000
Manager's profit-sharing at 10% of P&L profit		5000
Net profit after manager's profit-sharing, and before provision for income taxes		45,000

Here are some basic do's and don'ts in creating and managing profit centers:

1. The profit center should be easy to identify as a separate business where the manager has clear authority and responsibility.

2. The manager should be motivated by a leveraged or nonleveraged profit-sharing plan for his center.

3. Prepare P&Ls as often as possible, either weekly or monthly.

4. Never, never change a deal. If a manager is not performing, pull him out, but never alter a deal because the manager is making too much money.

5. Keep the plan simple and clear-cut.

6. Have your agreement in writing. A typical condition would be: "In the event of the manager's termination of employment, the bonus shall be computed and paid up to the last week of his/her employment." Have your attorney approve the agreement form.

7. Include recognition in rewarding your managers.

It might seem that recognition is something bestowed with ease, such as making your sales manager the vice-president in charge of marketing, and having some new business cards printed for him. This is OK, but it is not the true essence of recognition.

The secret of good recognition lies in a basic equation of business: responsibility equals authority. You must be willing to give your managers real responsibility, which means you must give them real authority. Making a key person a vice-president lacks substance unless it is coupled with real delegation of authority and responsibility. Of course, authority does not include giving a manager the opportunity to run amok. He surely will not be signing checks, for example. Your written agreement should clearly spell out where his authority lies and what its limits are.

8. Profit-center managers should report to supervisors who have had experience in the operation of the profit center. For example, the manager of one of our doughnut shops must be responsible to a supervisor who is experienced in every aspect of running that store. Nothing will take the wind out of the sails of a good manager faster than a supervisor who doesn't know his business. Our store managers respect their supervisors, because they have "been there" and understand the problems.

9. Don't leave a manager who is not doing a good job in a profit center. You are going to make some mistakes. In business there is always the risk of promoting a person to a level of incompetence. A classic example is making the star salesman the sales manager and finding he is a flop in that role; he has been promoted to a level of incompetence.

Look for the traits required in the management job. If you make a mistake in judgment, and a person clearly is not going to make it as a manager, you must promptly make a change. This ability to be objective in analyzing performance, and to act decisively when a person does not work out, will be a true test for the entrepreneur.

10. Always allow yourself good visibility into your profit centers, without sharing the responsibilities of the managers. If a manager is making mistakes or failing to follow through on his responsibilities, there is a natural tendency to jump in and help him. But this will muddy the waters of his responsibility because you are both involved. Keep good visibility and communication, but keep hands off the manager's job.

Don't be afraid to communicate deficiencies to the manager, or even to warn him that he is on probation and must clear up specific areas of poor performance if he is to stay. This open line of communication can save a situation and therefore save a manager from downfall. Give him an opportunity to clear up his problems by telling him up front what you expect and where you see inadequacies.

Successful implementation of profit centers will enable you to profitably multiply your own effort and enlarge your business. A well-motivated manager will be like a partner to you, and his success will insure yours also. Can profit centers be applied to your business? This will depend on your desire to multiply your own effort, and also on your ability to design profit centers that work.

26
HOW TO BUY

You already are an experienced buyer. You have been buying groceries and clothes and cars and homes. This lifetime of experience, however, doesn't qualify you to buy for your business any more than your experience at eating in restaurants qualifies you to become a restaurateur.

How you buy can make the difference between having a controlled operation or a fiasco, and it requires skill and discipline. Inappropriate buying is usually one of the major causes when a business loses financial equilibrium. For example, the purchasing of capital equipment without cash flow analysis or without adequate contractual safeguards can result in catastrophic losses. Your buying must be accomplished within controlled, defined rules. Utilize each and every one of the following policies. They come from experience.

POLICIES ON HOW TO BUY

1. Buy hand to mouth.
2. Use an inventory control system.
3. Pay on time.
4. Be loyal to good suppliers.
5. Count and inspect everything when received.
6. Ask for and take term discounts.
7. Get price protection.
8. Award to the lowest bidder.
9. Purchase orders must be in writing.
10. Squeaky wheels get oiled.
11. Never order anything without knowing the price first.
12. Have backup sources.
13. Have complete specifications.

14. Ask for concessions.
15. Pull, don't push.
16. Have promises verified in writing.
17. Get construction work bonded.
18. Extras must be approved in writing prior to the work.
19. Use internal controls for ordering and receiving.
20. Pay after verification.
21. Communicate complaints.
22. Buy subject to your contingencies.
23. Romance your suppliers.
24. Watch your cash flow.
25. Suppliers can be a source of financing.

Let's take a closer look at these rules. Item 1 advises you never to buy larger quantities than you need. Buy hand to mouth. The price of a product will be less if you buy a larger quantity, so there is always a tendency to buy more than you need. But there are practical reasons to resist this temptation. It will harm your liquidity because you are tying up more cash. Also, merchandise has a tendency to become obsolete before you even imagine it to be possible. You will also tie up storage space with the extra amount you buy. Altogether, it just doesn't make good sense.

Item 2 calls for an inventory control system. You will need a standard procedure to follow, and your accountant can help in deciding what will work best. We use a "build-to" system. Every item in stock is assigned a "build-to" quantity. When merchandise is ordered, the amount to buy is determined by counting what is in stock and ordering a quantity that will build the total to the "build-to" maximum.

Item 3: Pay on time. Successful business people have a reputation for dependability with their suppliers. If your suppliers can depend on you for prompt payment, you can depend on them when you need them. Paying on time is the greatest single tool you have in buying. With it, you can demand and get better prices, services, and promptness from your suppliers. If for any reason you cannot pay on time, review Chapter 27, "How To Borrow Money," and Chapter 29, "When Your Feet Are in the Fire."

Item 4: Be loyal to good suppliers. Successful people have long relationships with their suppliers. This is strong evidence of a mutually supportive relationship, one that has been good for both parties. Sometimes long relationships are an outgrowth of having a supplier stay with the business during its early, difficult times.

During periods of short supply, a seller's market, suppliers will be loyal to good customers. Sometimes they are slow in deliveries due to expanded demand for their product, but a good supplier will again be loyal to a good customer.

Item 5 advises "Count and inspect everything when received." Can you imagine how a grocery store could function if this policy were not followed? The next time you're at the market, see if you can spot the bread man or other supplier standing with his cart of merchandise, waiting to be counted before entering the store. If a grocery store requires this basic control, surely you should too. Count everything you receive and verify the count against the receiving document, your purchase order, and the invoice. Have the delivery person sign for any discrepancies.

Item 6: Ask for and take term discounts. A typical term discount might be 2 percent ten days, net thirty days. Let's assume that a supplier's normal terms are net thirty days. You might take the initiative by asking for 2 percent ten-day terms. This is a significant savings that justifies having your cash flow set up to provide cash just for this purpose.

Item 7: Get price protection. During inflationary times, when placing an order it is worth added effort to specify that the price will be good for a stated period of time. Let's assume you operate a store that sells jelly beans. If you buy 100 pounds of jelly beans every month, you might place a fixed-price purchase order for 1200 pounds (at the 1200-pound price), with monthly shipments of 100 pounds. In this way you accomplish two benefits, a lower price and one-year price protection. Your ordering terms should provide that in the event prices decrease, you would be billed at the lower price.

Item 8: Award to the lowest bidder. Always get bids. It is the only way to assure you are buying at the lowest price. Also, you must keep regular suppliers honest by periodically having bids taken on their merchandise. When comparing bids, obviously you must exercise judgment in comparing specifications.

Give the order to the supplier who is the successful bidder. This may or may not be the low bidder, if other terms or quality differences offset the lowest price. The only reasons not to let a contract to the low bidder would be that he is unqualified or has not bid on a comparable basis. Don't play games with the lowest bidder. He bought his ticket in his willingness to compete and should therefore be rewarded. This policy will result in suppliers' providing their best prices from the first, because they know you will award the job to the lowest bidder every time.

Giving the order to the lowest bidder may seem to contradict a previous item, be loyal to good suppliers. Separate purchases made on the basis of bidding from those made without bidding. You may have suppliers whose competitiveness is maintained without receiving bids. Or you may be buying proprietary products from a source that has no competitors. When you do resort to bidding, however, you should make it clear to all that you are going to give the order to the lowest bidder.

Item 9 is a basic: Purchase orders must be in writing. This policy will avoid numerous misunderstandings and errors. Spell out every condition of the purchase, including the shipping instructions, who pays the freight, and terms.

Item 10: Squeaky wheels get oiled. At times you will be in a seller's market, and you will have to hustle to maintain your flow of incoming goods. When delivery is slow, apply your own selling ability. This is when you must be assertive. During periods of shortage, the customers who keep up the pressure are those who receive the best treatment. Sometimes a supplier will satisfy a nagging customer just to escape the hassle.

Item 11 is a fundamental: Never order anything without knowing the price first. This rule is taken for granted in large purchases. It is more easily overlooked in the small purchase or repair order, or where labor is the major cost. It is human nature to be trusting. Also, it seems nice to authorize some small job and depend on the supplier's sense of fairness. However, it absolutely does not work as an ongoing business policy. Every time you authorize work without a quotation in advance, you pay more than if you get a price.

Lawyers and accountants charge on an hourly basis. Have a discussion with them regarding hourly fees before you begin your relationship. While you must accept their principle of working on an hourly basis, have them give you their estimate of the number of hours to complete the job at hand (say, an audit). Then, suggest this be used as a "not to exceed" maximum. This will avoid the open-end approach in which the CPA, in the absence of an estimate, simply incurs hours without restraint.

Item 12 recommends that you have backup sources. In order to get lower prices, you may buy from only one source. This matter of concentrating purchases is a business decision. To the degree that you limit the number of suppliers, it becomes important to have backup sources. Suppliers can be shut down for all kinds of reasons, including strikes, shortages, and unpredictable events.

There are a number of ways to maintain backup sources. The most foolproof is to have more than one source initially, to split the business. Another is to keep backup sources informed and friendly; let them appreciate the loyalty you have toward your primary supplier.

Item 13: Have complete specifications. There is only one way to be specific and that is in writing. In letting a contract for a building, it would be foolhardy to proceed without a written set of plans and specifications. Use the written word to describe all aspects of a purchase too.

Great football teams succeed because of their mastery of fundamentals, coupled with knowing how to avoid mistakes. Mistakes can needlessly impair the opportunity for victory. Who needs penalties? You surely don't when you start a business, and one way to eliminate mistakes is to be clear in important matters. Surely this applies to purchasing. Incidentally, you have just been given the secret to success in your own business—have a mastery of the fundamentals and don't make mistakes.

Item 14 suggests that you ask for concessions. There is a fine line between driving a hard bargain and asking for terms that cut off a good supplier. Remember, if you lose your good suppliers, you are left with bad ones. Also, by asking for terms that are unreasonable, you lose deals you really should have made. For example, in negotiating for a new store location, it would be damaging to be too tough, because you just would not reach an agreement. You would lose the benefits that the site would have provided.

On the other hand, the role of the buyer is to negotiate for the best price and terms that are available. Some shy people may feel uneasy in the role of purchasing agent. It is an opportunity to test your assertiveness: step right up and ask for concessions.

Item 15 advises you to pull, not push. This is the old spaghetti truism: it is easier to pull spaghetti than to push it. The same is true of your suppliers. Pushing them around is simply not productive from a business standpoint. It will only result in a continuous turnover of suppliers. Also, business dealings should be pleasant and stimulating, as well as a means of accomplishing your goals. If your relationship with a supplier is a good one, you will be better informed on industry trends, competition, and your own operations. A supplier who is a friend will be more inclined to be constructively critical and to advise you on specific problems that he can observe better than you. Also, remember there are always two possible conditions when you deal with a supplier. It's either a buyer's market or it's a seller's market. Suppliers with whom you have friendships will support you during a seller's market.

Item 16 advises "Have promises verified in writing." Handshake promises are fine, provided you understand one serious flaw: people forget. And human nature being what it is, we always seem to remember what we have coming but forget what we have promised. People without a crooked hair on their head may honestly sometimes forget just what they have promised. Therefore, if you have been given some promise in negotiations, write it down as one of the terms of the purchase order. Tell the supplier why you do so. It is not that you don't trust him to honor his word; it is just that you have to write things down to keep them straight.

Item 17 says "Get construction work bonded." This rule applies if you're having any substantial amount of construction work done. Usually, on a construction project you use a general contractor. Have him furnish you a lien and completion bond from an insurance company that meets with the approval of your lawyer or insurance agent.

Item 18 states that extras must be approved in writing prior to the work. This would apply, typically, to construction. The best protection against contractors who violate this rule is to have it spelled out in your purchase order. Again, this emphasizes the importance of the simplest equation in buying: control = written agreement.

Item 19 calls for internal controls for ordering and receiving. Your CPA can help establish a complete program, including forms to use, dividing responsibility between purchasing and receiving, and internal checks and balances to verify prices, quantities ordered, what was received, and other aspects of the transaction. Even large sophisticated businesses have run into disasters from dishonesty because they failed to install basic internal controls.

Item 20 says "Pay after verification." Sometimes suppliers hustle their customers into paying invoices before work is checked. A vendor will have greater respect for you if you tell him clearly that the invoice will not be paid until proper approval of the work is completed.

Item 21: Communicate complaints. One of the problems with restaurants is that they don't get many complaints because customers do not want to experience unpleasantness. The path of least resistance is to go away quietly but unhappily and not come back. This is why a good restaurant owner carefully watches the plates that come back to the kitchen, to spot which food is left untouched. He has to find out where his problems are from the plates, because his customers are not about to let him know.

While you may not want to complain in a restaurant, you must speak up loudly and clearly if you have problems with merchandise or service. When you do find faulty goods, don't wait to receive a credit memo from the supplier; immediately enter the credit in your own books, and deduct the amount from outstanding invoices.

Your suppliers will also benefit from your complaints, just as much as the owner of the restaurant would. Complaints build friendship and support from your suppliers, and not antagonism. If your complaints irritate a supplier or if he is not responsive to them, then make a change.

Item 22: Buy subject to your contingencies. Sometimes you may want to place an order even though information is incomplete, or put deadlines on delivery, or specify tolerances. The proper technique is to place an order that contains a contingency. For example, "This order is subject to the contingency that it be shipped by July first," or "This order is subject to the contingency that the widgets ordered have a fat content of a minimum of 20 percent and not to exceed 30 percent." Don't rely on assumptions. Put teeth into your purchase orders in the form of contingencies.

Item 23 says "Romance your suppliers." If your business is growing, as it should be, you can sometimes lower your costs by romancing your suppliers. For example, while we are purchasing merchandise now for ninety stores, we keep suppliers aware that new stores are in construction and others being planned. The supplier, therefore, can see the prospects of greater volume in the future and will be more inclined to give us lower prices now.

Item 24: Watch your cash flow. Everything you buy creates a disbursement of cash that must be part of your cash flow control. If you are buying a capital item such as fixtures or machinery, you must be satisfied that your cash flow can safely handle the obligation created. When you buy merchandise or raw material used in the products you sell, you must be sure that cash equilibrium is maintained so that these purchases can be paid for on time. The liquidity of your business can be upset by imprudent buying.

Finally, your suppliers can be a source of financing. Item 25 on our list is covered in Chapter 27. If you wish to use a supplier as a source of financing, first develop a track record with him, using normal terms. When the supplier gains confidence in you, and you have a record of meeting standard terms, he will have a much better basis to extend terms and thereby create financing for you. The other alternative is that a good track record of prompt payment to one supplier would encourage a new supplier to go a step further and extend additional terms.

For your own business, you might want to review "Policies on How to Buy" on pages 183–84 from time to time. This will insure you're not slipping out of control in good buying procedures.

27

HOW TO BORROW MONEY

The entrepreneur who borrows money uses one of the oldest known tools of man, the lever. Leverage is at work when you buy a $100,000 house with a $50,000 mortgage and $50,000 cash. The mortgage provides you with the lever, or the ability to acquire a $100,000 house, even though your cash is only $50,000. You are 50 percent leveraged.

The principle is also a simple equation: leverage equals risk. The higher the leverage, the higher the risk. When you borrow money, obviously you must agree to pay it back. The risk created by borrowing stems from the fact that the lender will not be satisfied with only your promise to pay him back. He will want assurance, or security.

When you buy a house with a mortgage, what happens if you break your promise to pay back your mortgage? You lose your house and the $50,000 that went into it. The lever has just swung back and knocked you right out of the saddle.

When you borrow, you create leverage by the use of OPM: Other People's Money. It can be in the form of loans or capital. If others put capital into your company, they become stockholders.

On the other hand, if the OPM is in the form of loans, you are obviously in an entirely different relationship. You are obligated to pay the money back with interest. You have the responsibility, before borrowing, to be sure you have the cash flow to repay on time.

It is my recommendation that all of your OPM be in the form of loans and not capital. You should furnish all of the capital in a sufficient amount to make your business work. Your own capital will be used for items such as inventories, working capital, and start-up costs. This money stays in your enterprise.

There are a number of reasons not to have OPM in the form of capital. It may be difficult to sell stock in your business, and you need approval from the corporations commissioner of your state. Also, when you sell stock you have diluted ownership. Now you must report to stockholders. There are exceptions, of course, to the rule of "Don't sell stock." For example, no one would start a steel mill without investor capital. The suggestions about borrowing money that follow assume you are dealing with lenders and not investors.

A growing company may need to borrow money, and here are some broad rules about leveraging your expansion with OPM. The first rule is not to borrow at all unless there is a compelling reason to do so.

Do not use OPM unless the benefits of the money will result in a predictable source of repayment. Just because it is OPM, that doesn't mean it makes sense to spend $5000 on a new machine if a $2000 used machine will do the same job. This is especially true in a start-up situation in which your source of repayment is not so clearly assured. Keep your debt to an austere minimum.

The art of borrowing money is a skill that disproves the old tale, "The only time you can get a loan is when you don't need one." You really can borrow money if you know how to go about it. Borrowing money successfully (including repayment) separates the big winners from the big losers in business. The big winners are successful in exercising leverage and therefore multiplying success. The losers, if leveraged, probably lose it all.

The winner is at one extreme and the loser is at the other. In between are the ones who didn't borrow at all. They are not big winners because they didn't use the leverage of borrowing. But on the other hand, they are not losers either, because they didn't incur the risk of borrowing. To the extent that these people do borrow, they move to the winning or losing side, depending on their success or failure in handling leverage.

You normally have only one principal lender, your banker.

His sense of security is hampered if you owe money to another bank. Also, a banker is usually reluctant to make loans unless his bank is handling the accounts of the borrower. The key is to deal with a banker who individually has the lending authority to take care of your anticipated loan needs. You should deal with the man who runs the store.

Frank and I were turned down once on a loan request involving a new warehouse. Our business was five years old at the time. We had been with a small branch of a large bank for the entire five-year period. Our business had grown over those five years, and it was our first large request for a loan. The bank manager did not have the authority to make the loan and the decision had to be made "downtown" by someone who knew nothing about our business other then our financial statement. We were turned down by someone we had never met.

Sell the sizzle to your banker. Our business is concentrated in the morning hours. If you go into a doughnut shop at three o'clock in the afternoon, you may not see a single customer. But at 8:30 any morning you will smell the doughnuts being made and see lots of customers having a pleasant experience. We make sure that our banker sees our stores at 8:30 in the morning. That's the sizzle. We also make sure the bank has samples of our doughnuts from time to time so office workers can remind the manager just how good those doughnuts are. Our business lends itself to sizzle, right? But so does yours, and you have to sell it.

Another way to create sizzle is to get your banker involved. Make a point of inviting him out to your place of business. Let him experience the sights, sounds, and smells of your operation. Bankers enjoy getting out of their offices, and these visits will clear up questions they may not have expressed.

When you borrow, ask for a bit more than you need. To do this, you will have to push through a normal barrier, the tendency to ask for less than you need. The reason most of us ask for less is that we think the less we ask for, the greater is our chance of getting the loan. But having a loan of more than you need will cover unanticipated costs and improve your ability to make loan payments on time.

Don't let the banker think you are growing fast. And absolutely never use rapid growth as a selling point (even if you *are* growing fast). Rapid growth turns a banker off faster than almost anything, and perhaps rightly so. The reason is simple. Businesses that grow at a slow rate are usually better controlled and result in safer loans than rapidly growing businesses. In a rapid-growth situation the emphasis should be on your proven ability to control the operation at the speed you are going, and not on the speed itself.

Don't schedule repayment of your loan at too fast a clip. If you need a loan for thirty days, ask for ninety days. If your forecast proves correct and you can pay in thirty days, do so even though you asked for and got ninety days. You are then a hero to your banker. On the other hand, if you borrowed on a thirty-day basis and found you could not repay until ninety days, you are a problem to your banker.

Some years ago, I was in a business meeting and one of the participants was a man named Charlie. When it was Charlie's turn to present his views, he resorted to more and more exaggerations in order to make his points. Finally, one of his coworkers couldn't stand it any more and admonished: "Charlie, if I've told you once I've told you a million times, don't exaggerate!"

Exaggeration is easy to detect when we hear it from others. Yet it is such an available tool to embellish arguments that sometimes we indulge in it ourselves, not realizing the listener picks it up for just what it is. When we talk to a lender, we know his decision is going to be based essentially on numbers. It is so easy for us to exaggerate them in our conversation, and so easy for him to pick up our exaggerations.

So, when borrowing money, don't exaggerate. Don't exaggerate your sales or profits or forecasts. Don't fail to disclose problem areas of your business. Don't overstate your ability to repay loans. Whatever is told to a lender that is not accurate will come back to impair the most important asset you are trying to build with him, your credibility.

What you should sell is credibility plus sizzle. Credibility means you are for real and this, together with sizzle, results in the lender's selling himself to you rather than the other way around. At Yum Yum, our lenders, especially leasing companies, compete for our business. The reason is that my partner, Frank Watase, has convinced them with credibility plus sizzle.

Let's assume you wish to leverage your particular business. Some businesses offer greater opportunities than others. Real estate development or construction usually give more leverage possibilities because of traditionally available financing, in the form of mortgages.

What other sources are there? When opening a new store, there are financing possibilities that have no connection with your bank. The company that installs electric signs will finance through their own bank. This is recourse financing. If you fail to make payments on the signs, the sign company's bank looks to them for recourse.

Commercial leasing companies finance store equipment. If you become involved with equipment leasing, bring in your lawyer and accountant to approve the terms and insure that you receive benefits such as investment tax credit. Some equipment can be financed directly by the manufacturer. So, rather than use up your line of credit, you can purchase equipment with built-in financing.

Another source that is a powerful generator of cash is financing from suppliers. Let us assume your monthly purchases are $25,000 and the normal terms of payment are thirty days. Now, if your supplier will give sixty-day terms, you have improved your cash flow at a zero rate of interest.

For those who highly leverage their businesses, the uncovering of new sources of financing becomes an intriguing game. One way to stimulate your thinking is to keep a list of all possible sources you can imagine. While you have only one banker, you might keep a list of alternate bankers you would contact if your present one turns you down. Incidentally, if you do get turned down, talk to only one other banker at a time. Let the potential new banker know this, and have him agree to give you an answer within a specific period of time.

Make up another list of lenders, other than bankers, who can become an ever growing army of backup supporters if and when you need them. This list might include individuals, suppliers, leasing companies, equipment sources, cigarette vending companies, landlords, mortgage lenders, and even your mother-in-law.

Different lenders supply different kinds of needs. Your banker should be reserved for in-and-out borrowing as indicated by your cash flow requirements. Suppliers, by selling on extended terms, furnish working capital. Major pieces of equipment can be financed with long-term loans that relate to the life of the equipment. Keep your list in an ongoing file of lenders that you constantly revise and expand.

A landlord furnishing special improvements normally amortizes these costs over the length of your lease. If your improvements in a building cost $10,000 and you sign a five-year lease, you are expected to pay, in addition to the rent on the building, an additional $2000 per year for five years to reimburse the landlord for the improvements.

If you have your annual audit certified by your CPA, it can be an extremely valuable tool in selling your company to lenders. A certified statement includes a report signed by the CPA that the audit was performed in accordance with standard accounting principles. It gives the lender an outside, universally accepted verification that the financial report is an accurate one. A certified statement is expensive; remember the CPA is putting his signature on the line that the statement is accurate.

Timing is an important element in borrowing money. Don't get caught up in the air with an empty gas tank. Your cash flow tells you when your tank will be empty. You must have your borrowing approved by the lender *before* the need, not at the time of need.

Let's assume your cash flow shows a need for borrowing in July. Talk to your banker about it in March. Get him to approve your loan early enough so that if he turns you down you still have enough time to look for another lender. Your cash flow will impress on the banker that you are prudent and also knowledgeable in finance. It gives him assurance that you are keeping your eye on liquidity, which he has a very keen interest in, especially if some of his money is in your business.

Be prepared in advance to handle the two big questions your lender has on his mind: "Why do you need the money?" and "What is your source of repayment?" Never go to a banker unless you have precise answers to these questions. You should not only have details about your source of repayment, but you should also be prepared to give him alternate sources such as other income, other collateral, or whatever is appropriate and available.

In dealing with your banker or other lender, the trick is for you to accept his interest rate and for him to accept your wishes as to repayment time. What he charges you in interest is somewhat controlled by what he charges everybody else, but the length of time to repay is not. And this is important to you, because a longer period of repayment can be handled much easier by your cash flow. In other words, give your banker the interest rate he wants, but strive valiantly for a long repayment period. If you need sixty days to pay, ask for 120.

You have been learning how to expand your business through OPM. There is another rule that goes hand in hand with what you've learned. Don't tie up capital in the general category of "fixed assets," which drain your working capital strength. Lease your office or factory or store rather than buy. Finance your car and furniture. Leverage is increased by minimizing investment in anything you use. Keep liquid, keep lean, and borrow only when there is an absolutely clear and sensible reason to do so. You want to be sure that when you do borrow, the money results in sufficient profit and cash flow to service the debt.

Finally, the real essence of borrowing money is having good credibility, as judged by your track record. Your ability to borrow, then, is a self-determined element. If you are dealing with a banker, and your history has been one of not repaying loans on time, you have made it very difficult for him to lend you money again.

The entrepreneur who has experienced a past bankruptcy has a really serious credibility problem when dealing with lenders. To begin with, personal credit history is now tracked by computers with long memories. My company is the largest privately owned retail doughnut-shop chain in the United States. Yet our Dun and Bradstreet Report still spells out my personal bankruptcy fourteen years after the event.

I have two suggestions on how to deal with a prior bankruptcy when you make contact with a banker. First, disclose it to him up front and explain the circumstances. The alternative is for him to find out by reading your credit history. This unpleasant surprise will lead the lender to draw his own and most likely unfavorable conclusions.

My second suggestion may seem somewhat harder to swallow. You should show your banker that once you became capable of doing so, you began making good on those bankruptcy debts. It might have taken you a long time to start (as it did me), but it will be the ultimate signal of credibility to your banker.

Yum Yum Donut Shops recently received an $8,000,000 line of credit from Wells Fargo Bank. The loan request had been turned down when my earlier bankruptcy resurfaced. When the bank learned of payments I had begun to make to those bankruptcy creditors, the loan was reconsidered and approved.

In your own business you will have ongoing relationships with all kinds of creditors. As you grow, you will be asking these people for more credit. If you go to a creditor and ask for extended terms, his answer depends on whether you have been slow to pay in the past. If your experience with him has been one of always paying on time, then you have a reasonable chance of his considering your request for extended terms.

So, the key in building your ability to borrow is to always pay on time—even if you have to borrow to do it.

28
SALES TALK

The free enterprise system is the most formidable economic force in the world, and the catalyst that makes it work is competition. The freedom that enables you to go into business obviously permits everyone else to do it too.

It has been said that warfare does not determine who is right—but who is left. To survive in business, your battles will be for customers who are sought after by earnest and often more experienced competitors. Irrespective of what business you start, survival goes to the fittest and the fittest are those who succeed in merchandising their product or service.

Merchandising is a joining of forces that produce sales. These forces might include advertising, pricing, promotion, display, product benefits, and an endless variety of other inducements that create sales. This chapter offers some suggestions that will make you aware of the importance of merchandising, and also stimulate you to create your own plan.

To begin, there is one overall approach that I earnestly

recommend because it is foolproof. Use the merchandising methods that have already proven to be most successful in your own particular business. You are free to copy, if you will, those who have done the best. Play the winners.

Different businesses have their own most effective merchandising techniques. Within your business there is probably a successful established pattern that may have emerged after a great deal of trial and error. If you study the most successful people in your own business, you can identify this pattern. Thus your first step is to determine from successful competitors the exact combination of selling tools that works best. There is absolutely no percentage in galloping off in a different direction.

This is sometimes easier said than done. If you go into the doughnut business and you are a former advertising man, your inclination will be to follow the promotional methods you found successful in selling, let us say, toothpaste. I have seen some intelligent people fail in the doughnut business for this reason. They focus their attention on methods that work in another business rather than concentrating on the merchandising methods that work for doughnuts. You must identify what is right for your own business.

Assume that you want to start building speculative houses. How are you going to sell them? Easy—copy the most successful speculative builder that you know. Is there a certain floor plan that he has found successful? Is his price range one that sells? Determine the key elements of his success and use them. If he uses open houses, then you use open houses. If he sells through broker X, then you sell through broker X. If he runs ads in the *Tribune* listing features of his houses, then you do the same. If he uses Mrs. Jones as a color coordinator, you use Mrs. Jones too. Find out, and use those selling tools that have already been successful.

The real key to successful selling is your product. If a product is uniquely good, it removes itself from competition. You must have clear goals about the nature of the product itself, including quality, size, value, and benefits.

There are some businesses in which promotional and advertising effort play a secondary role, and it is important to recognize them. The classic example is food. Restaurant merchandising is done by the quality of the food and the operation itself. If a restaurant maintains optimum quality, is spotlessly clean, and has a friendly crew, it will draw customers from others with lesser quality, irrespective of their efforts to attract customers by promotional or advertising efforts.

What would happen to a start-up restaurant owner who advertised before his quality was established? He unknowingly would put himself into a downward spiral, with the following sequence. With the emphasis on promotion, his concentration would no longer entirely focus on quality. His menu might be inferior to that of his competitor, who concentrates all effort on quality. The public will respond to his promotional effort and come into his restaurant, but they experience an average meal or an inferior one. The public will immediately write off the new restaurant and accelerate its downfall.

What I have stated here is that a good meal sells itself, and that is not true for most products or services. In most cases, you must design an overall merchandising plan to sell your products. I suggest you keep one basic goal in mind: sell in volume. Think in terms of selling your product in large quantities. There are some compelling reasons to take this approach.

The first is that fixed costs represent an increasing percentage of total costs. For example, the cost of electricity is increasing at a rate that exceeds that of the cost of living. All of the mushrooming fixed costs must be absorbed by sales. Today and in the future, businesses must gear up to greater volumes in order to spread fixed costs over a greater volume of sales. If you start a business on the theory of "thinking small," your fixed costs as a percentage of your sales can eat you up alive.

Another reason to approach merchandising with a goal of high volume is that this normally results in greater values to your customers. Offering a greater value is your key to a high level of sales. The best examples we have today of successful businesses are ones in which the customer receives a high value: that's the secret of how large businesses become large. Think for a minute about restaurants that are so successful they are in a class by themselves; those for which you expect to find customers waiting out on the sidewalk. They are the ones that give a good value.

A high value does not necessarily increase costs. I am referring to overall costs as a percentage of sales. In the case of a restaurant, the sum of the cost of labor and merchandise is the important total. For example, assume that a restaurant operates on a labor cost of 30 percent and a food cost of 30 percent. If this restaurant were to improve the value it gives to its customers, it would serve greater quantities or higher quality food, or both. Let us suppose that to give a better value, the food cost is increased from 30 percent to 36 percent. This means that the customer is now receiving 20 percent more value. Keep in mind that the overall cost has gone up only 6 percent, from 30 percent of 100 percent to 36 percent of 100 percent. Does this mean that the owner operates with 6 percent less profit? Probably not. Actually, the owner may operate at a higher profit without increasing his total costs at all.

If you think this is a riddle, it is not. The answer lies in the fact that the owner has decided to give 20 percent more value to his customers. The normal effect would be that he will have more customers, and the result of more customers is that his labor cost will go down. If, due to his higher volume, his labor cost is reduced from 30 percent to 24 percent, his overall costs have not changed at all. Furthermore, the higher level of sales will lower other costs. Let's assume sales go from $100 to $150 as a result of offering greater value. The rent cost at $150 of sales is a smaller percentage than what it would be at $100 of sales.

By offering greater value, higher sales and profits are achieved. If you still don't quite accept this, think again of any successful business with which you are familiar. They probably offer an especially good value, and operate at a high level of sales.

Personally get involved in the selling end of your business. Become an expert in selling. If you are not comfortable as a salesperson, it is still helpful to learn the fundamentals of salesmanship from the vast assortment of "how to sell" books, including ones that cover your own particular field.

Learning to sell your product results in some extra benefits. You learn a great deal about your customers, including finding out what they want and what they don't want. Input from customers is your most important source of information and ideas. When you deal with customers, you are at the heart of your business, the point of sale. You are in touch with what is right and what is wrong in your business. It is incredible how you, as owner, can pick up ways to improve your operation by contact with customers.

I have spent a great many hours waiting on customers. Each time I learn something new. Just recently one of our designers recommended that we no longer use hand sinks in the back bar area of future stores. This is the area where coffee is made. My experience in selling doughnuts had taught me the importance of that sink for rinsing coffeepots and bar towels. My selling experience made the decision easy—we still use the sink.

Your own selling experience in your business will be valuable in setting up a sales organization. For one, you will have a realistic view of what can be expected of salespeople. The best salespeople are the ones who are interested in a commission form of incentive. Obviously, there is an infinite variety of ways to structure commission compensation. This is an area for you to exercise ingenuity in, to design a plan for your sales force that results in happy and highly motivated personnel. Find out how your successful competitors structure their sales organizations.

There are many different tools you can work with to sell your product, and many of them can be used concurrently in order to get the best results. Here are some pointers:

1. Open your new business quietly, to allow your personnel to train and properly tune up. Once everything is smooth, then hold your grand opening. You want customers at a grand opening to have a pleasant experience so they will come back. Nothing could be worse than to have throngs come to a grand opening and receive poor service from untrained help.

2. There is a whole chapter in this book on the subject of location (Chapter 23). In a great percentage of all retail businesses, success or failure depends on location.

3. Have professional decor. Find a specialist for your own kind of business. For example, there are specialized firms that do nothing except restaurant decor. Professional decor makes for a pleasant experience for your customers and will bring them back. Decor can be coordinated with all the other visual aspects of your business, such as stationery, signs, architecture, packaging, and surely your products.

4. Sell the senses. The fragrance of a real bakery is one of the compelling reasons people like to trade there. You may need to use some imagination to see if the sense of sight or touch or smell can be applied to help you merchandise your product.

5. Signs are important. Get them as big as you can afford, within the limits of city ordinances and your lease. Keep the copy down to a minimum. Sometimes signs look like brochures. Don't get so cute with your copy or business name that it obscures what business you are in. Pick a business name that is easy to remember. If your name has a visual image, people will be more inclined to remember it. One of our best business assets is our name, because so many people have chuckled over its appropriateness: Yum Yum Donuts.

6. Complement your own talents. If you're production-oriented, bring in a sales manager who is a real pro in your type of business. If your capability lies in sales, bring in a production manager to complement the area of your own expertise.

7. Light up your store. Lights advertise your presence and make people feel welcome and secure. Use time clocks to avoid burning lights and signs when they are not needed. Electricity is very expensive, so use fluorescent fixtures rather than incandescent bulbs, and you get five times more light for your dollar. Also, fluorescent tubes have a longer life than incandescent and your maintenance cost will be reduced.

8. Attract customers with sales. A sale can bring in a new customer who, if pleased, will become a permanent one.

9. Publicity may be appropriate in some businesses. The greatest risk is that business owners become enamored of publicity and forget the fundamentals, which are of paramount importance.

10. Proper displays are an important tool for you. See how the professionals do it in your business and pick up their ideas. Special holiday decor pleases and motivates your customers. Create displays that make it easy for them to make a decision to buy.

11. Packaging is a part of your overall image. Your boxes, bags, and other forms of packaging continue to sell for you after they leave your store. Your decor consultant can help you in this.

12. Celebrity identification is not normally useful for a business. As a rule, this kind of a tie-in usually connotes a promotional approach. Are you really turned on by a restaurant because it carries the name of a pro football player? Probably not.

13. There may be an opportunity for demonstration to be used in your merchandising plan. We all know that vacuum cleaners are sold in Sears stores by demonstration. In a clothing store, the best salespeople get customers to try on clothes. They get the customers involved. Within the limits of good taste and judgment, employ those forms of demonstration that make sales.

14. Some selling requires a professional presentation and close. There is absolutely no way that encyclopedias could be sold without a precisely conceived pitch and close. If your business is one in which professional selling is required, have a fine-tuned, professional sales approach rather than a helter-skelter one.

15. Training is an ongoing requirement in a sales force. Have periodic sessions with your sales force to review products and sales techniques. These meetings can be used to motivate your salespeople too. Use agendas that are tight and controlled to make sales meetings exciting events.

16. Advertise only in the media that work best for your business. Learn to say no to the constant barrage you will receive from advertising salesmen in other media. You don't have the time or money to experiment, and surely not because of the pitch of an advertising salesman. Watch your overall advertising budget. Keep it within proper limits when measured as a percentage of sales.

17. When you do advertise, be sure not to use unprofessional ads or promotions. Nothing turns off a customer quicker than a silly ad. There is a great deal of money misspent in advertising that attempts to be funny. Not many humorous ads work for the benefit of the advertiser, especially in small business. Your advertising money is meant to bring customers in, and it doesn't make sense to spend it when it does not accomplish its goal.

The greatest safeguard against silly ads is to use professional help. Find an advertising agency with experience in your field, one you feel comfortable with. Be straightforward and consistent in your ads. One of my favorite advertisers is Home Savings and Loan in California: year after year they pound home the same story, strength and safety.

In conclusion, I acknowledge that each one of us places a different emphasis on merchandising, based on our different backgrounds. Some are product- or production-oriented.

Others focus more on the merchandising aspects of operating a business. These differences also arise out of our individual strengths and personalities. If a person is production-oriented, he must learn and embrace merchandising tools until they become an acquired skill. On the other hand, if a person's background is merchandising, he must not allow it to overshadow the importance of the product itself.

Never operate a business without a profit, which is the nourishment your business needs to survive and grow. Don't become a victim of the old joke: "We lose money on every sale, but we make it up on volume." Pricing policy therefore becomes a critical aspect of your merchandising plans.

The first rule in pricing is to know your costs. If you need help, have your CPA assist in determining direct material, labor, and general and administrative costs. Usually the total direct cost, the sum of materials and labor, must be kept within a certain percentage of sales if a profit is to result. In some businesses, material costs dominate this total, and in others the labor cost will. If a restaurant were to operate with a total direct cost of say, 80 percent, there would never be a profit.

Pricing is influenced by competition. Some businesses can set prices without regard to those of competitors. These cases are rare indeed; most of us must acknowledge that the public is sensitive to price, and if we want to sell we must compete.

Pricing is the art of achieving balance between two opposing forces that must work together to succeed. One force is the importance of creating volume, which demands that your prices be low enough to attract more customers. The other force is the importance of making a profit. Some business owners fail because they sell too cheaply; others because they overprice merchandise. More fail because of underpricing than overpricing. The winners are those who hit the target of selling lots of merchandise at prices that result in profit for themselves and satisfaction to their customers.

29
WHEN YOUR FEET ARE IN THE FIRE

Remember the story of the famous last words of Samuel Upham, of Drew Theological Seminary? When his end was near, family and friends gathered at his bedside. The question arose as to whether he was still living or not. Someone advised, "Feel his feet. No one ever dies with warm feet." Then Dr. Upham opened an eye and said with a smile, "Joan of Arc did." Those were his last words.

You don't have to be Joan of Arc to have your feet in the fire. All entrepreneurs, at one time or another, find themselves in this condition. Business without problems is not business. The pendulum inevitably swings both ways, through good times and bad times.

This chapter deals with the ways to act when you have business problems. Not the normal day-to-day problems, but those that rock your equilibrium. Problems arise as a result of inadequate profits or poor cash flow, or both. How you perform during these periods determines your success in piloting your business through the storms and back into clear sailing again.

When we tell about our business disasters, it usually is somebody else's fault. If we were in business with a partner, it was the other guy who fouled up. If we were on our own, there was always some inescapable outside force that doomed us. There is a good deal of nonsense in most of these explanations. You can control events, including situations in which you are beset by difficulties. A great many disasters are caused by mishandled problems, and could be prevented by proper reaction during stressful times.

Watergate is surely one of the classic examples of how mishandling problems can result in disaster. Poor judgment in dealing with one problem resulted in greater problems

Worse judgment in handling the larger problems created even more serious ones, and it became a devastating chain reaction. Ultimately, poor judgment resulted in a President's resignation, and imprisonment for trusted aides.

When President-elect Jimmy Carter was selecting key aides, there was a right-hand man slated for an important White House staff job. The FBI's check on him revealed a background of financial irregularities, including bounced checks. His record eliminated him from the important job. He had been in the restaurant business and the business failed. While it was failing, checks were bounced, and he took restaurant receipts and replaced the bad checks with cash. The deficiency lay in how he handled his problems, not in the business failure itself.

Here was a man who had a bright and analytical mind during the presidential campaign. In spite of his intelligence and the qualities that made him a key presidential adviser, he did not know how to act when his feet were in the fire.

Learning how to handle problems, then, can be an expensive lesson. On the other hand, you can learn by others' mistakes. Absorb the "hard time" rules that are already proven. They will become your navigation chart through the rocks and shoals of your business life. They consist of four basic principles, plus a number of do's and don'ts. The four principles are:

1. Identify and acknowledge your problems. It may be cash flow, a drop in sales, higher costs, new competition, business recession, or incompetent or dishonest employees. It may be a combination of all kinds of factors. Once you know what the problems are and acknowledge them, you have accepted where you are, and can deal with your situation.

2. Reduce your losses. If you have cut yourself badly, the first thing you do is to stop the flow of blood with a tourniquet. Blood is to your body what money is to your business. If your sales or profits are down, cut your costs. Keep cutting them until you have regained equilibrium, and the outward flow of cash is stopped. There is a natural tendency to be optimistic in the face of adversity, and this may cause you to delay taking cost-cutting steps. If your business has suffered a reduction in sales, take bold and prompt steps to reduce your costs rather than to sail on in anticipation of future improvement. Under no circumstances should you maintain items of expense "for the future." You won't have a future if you cannot get through today.

3. Don't switch horses. Stick to your own business and do not flip into something else in which you do not have experience. It is only natural to want to escape when you have problems. The basic alternatives in a dangerous situation are either fight or flight. In business, unless you have a fatally defective situation, it is far better to stick with what you know best. Ride out the storm in your own boat without looking for another. I was in the construction business and was good at it. During a slump that caused problems, I jumped into another business with which I was not familiar. And with that, I jumped from a difficult situation into a disaster.

4. Hang in there, baby. One of my dear friends, Rudy Akre, is wise and experienced. He and his wife, Ethel, just celebrated their fiftieth wedding anniversary, so Rudy has had time to collect thoughts. During his lifetime, he learned more from one boxing coach than all of the other schooling put together. It was simple and absolutely foolproof advice. The coach taught Rudy that to win a boxing match you just have to do one thing: keep punching. No matter how tired or punished he was, he was told to keep punching. And Rudy did win; his opponents would know when to quit and Rudy would not. In business, those who keep punching are able to ride through the problem times into the good times.

Certain other techniques help when you're in trouble. First of all, don't cut quality or value. Do the opposite: improve quality and value to your customer. You know the fundamentals of your business; stick to them and don't rely on gimmicks to get your feet out of the fire. When we have a doughnut shop that is doing poorly, the best approach is simply to keep our attention on fundamentals and just do a better job.

I remember the second Yum Yum shop. The first one had been successful, and the second store was my first venture into a chain operation. The sales were disappointing and I was under the gun, operating at a loss and not having resources. I tried all kinds of innovations to bring up the sales. I sold wholesale doughnuts to catering truck operators. I sold one type of doughnut through grocery stores. These efforts, while well intended, just took my attention away from what I really should have been doing all along—becoming a better retail doughnut shop. Later, after I concentrated on fundamentals, the sales began to grow and the store prospered.

When you're in trouble, you may not be able to pay bills. If you cannot pay a creditor when his bill is due, take action. Don't wait for him to call you. If you cannot pay on time, take the initiative and call him. Explain that you cannot pay him on time. Tell him why you cannot, and then tell him when you will make payment.

Never make a promise that you cannot keep. If the creditor must wait ninety more days, tell him ninety. Don't tell him thirty days and not be able to meet that deadline. The goal is to maintain the cooperation of your creditors, to keep them on your side rather than create an adversary relationship. You already broke one promise, since you were not able to pay when due; now it is crucial that you keep your creditor's good will.

The fastest way you can turn a sympathetic creditor into a snarling predator is to send him a check that bounces. This may seem like a pretty dumb thing to do; but you would be surprised to know how many people, under the pressure of a hounding collector, will do just about anything to get rid of him. Be fair and be firm with your creditors. If you find the only way you can pay $100 is to pay $5 per month for 20 months, say so. Say it firmly, and by all means perform on your promise. You will be surprised to see that it works.

If your cash flow projection indicates a need for financing in six weeks, start your corrective planning now. You must modify cash flow to maintain liquidity. Make up a list of possible sources of financing and begin work on each one. Items on your "sources of financing" might include your banker, your suppliers, personal loans, refinancing of assets you have, financing receivables, collecting from receivables, accelerating your own terms of payment on merchandise you sell, and so on. You will find there is a wide variety of sources of financing, and many ways that cash flow can be improved. Review Chapter 27 on how to borrow money.

It is also helpful to list ways that you can cut costs and write in how many dollars each item contributes to cash flow. Modify your cash flow projection by including these savings along with cash you can generate from financing. Your compass to guide you through financially troubled waters is your cash flow projections. It is imperative to make whatever changes are necessary to maintain liquidity.

When you have business problems—and this may come as a surprise to you—watch for opportunities. Some of the greatest success stories involve entrepreneurs who, in the most adverse business climate, seized on opportunities that became the cornerstones of empires. Unless your business problems arise purely out of internal difficulties, you probably are suffering from a slump that affects your whole industry. When your business is bad for external reasons, look for the opportunities that bad times bring.

When I was a general contractor building apartments, a drastic slump took place. Apartment construction was reduced 80 percent in a period of two years. Mortgage lenders were besieged with foreclosures. Builders suddenly had very little to build. It was a bleak time for my business.

There were also fantastic opportunities. Many of the savings and loan associations that had financed apartments had taken them back in foreclosure proceedings. They did not want these buildings, and it was possible to acquire large apartment projects without any cash, just by assuming the first trust deeds. Later these properties became enormously valuable. So, when your feet are in the fire, remember it may also signal the time for opportunity.

Another rule applies for all seasons, both good times and bad. Conduct your relationships with friendly, kind words. Our tongues can be destructive instruments. As a business owner, you are in a position of authority as far as your employees and suppliers are concerned. Under stress it is so easy to bully people with angry or vulgar words. You especially need the loyalty of employees and suppliers when you're in difficulty. There is a good reason to always use words that are sweet and soft—someday you may be called upon to eat them.

When your business is in trouble, you may find yourself overworking, and the stressful nature of the storm will fatigue you. It is important that you be able to think clearly during this period. To do this you must be especially disciplined in taking care of yourself. In times of hardship, program your life as though you were in training for a heavyweight championship fight, and become totally disciplined:

1. *Sleep*: Do not settle for less than your standard requirement.
2. *Diet*: Maintain one of optimum balance.
3. *Drinking*: Be very careful to ration your allowances of grog.
4. *Exercise*: Health and doctor permitting, perform aerobic exercise at least four times a week.
5. *Unbend the bow*: Get away for at least one or two days a week.

It is not always easy to think clearly when you're in trouble. "When you're up to your armpits in alligators, it is hard to remember that the original objective was to clear the swamp." To maintain a broad perspective, devote a certain amount of business time to reviewing the viability and long-range implications of your business. Step back and ask whether you are really correct in the approach and operation of your business.

We tend to become defensive when in trouble. Have outside experts give you their appraisal of your operation and problems. Some possible consultants include your banker, CPA, lawyer, and others in your own line of business. You will be surprised how responsive and helpful people are when asked to objectively appraise your problems. Seek out these people and be responsive to their comments. You may get a consensus of opinion that you really should not be pursuing your line of business at all; that you are whipping a dead horse. It's even helpful to hear this sometimes, provided you can be open-minded and benefit from these views. Combine the forces of your own dedication and the advice of others to broaden, change, shift, or do whatever may be necessary to cure a defective business, and transform it into a successful one.

The following summary is your checklist in handling your business problems:

WHEN YOUR FEET ARE IN THE FIRE

Follow the basic principles:
1. Identify and acknowledge problems.
2. Reduce losses.
3. Don't switch horses.
4. Hang in there, baby.

In conclusion, handle problems by following certain rules that work. You must take the responsibility of controlling everything that goes on in your business . . . including your problems.

DO'S AND DON'TS

Do	Don't
1. Improve quality and value.	1. Send worthless checks.
2. Take the initiative with creditors.	2. Break promises to creditors.
3. Use cash flow control to maintain liquidity.	3. Become punchy from fatigue.
4. Look for opportunities.	4. Overlook spiritual support.
5. Use soft words.	5. Delay necessary actions.
6. Maintain physical fitness.	
7. Have outsiders review your problems.	
8. Keep broad perspectives.	

STEP FIVE

PUT IT ALL TOGETHER

The entrepreneur, a rare and achieving individual, can expand to broader goals than those measured by balance sheets, recognition, and reward. There is much more. . . .

30

SHOEMAKER, STICK TO THY LAST

In this final section, "Put It All Together," we will look at being in your own business from a broad perspective. Business success is futile unless our lives make sense. What is the point of success unless we are happy and useful to the world? Once we have gained our beachhead in business, there are ways to insure success in our lives. These final chapters offer some suggestions.

Being in your own business is a different way of life. You are in control. Outside circumstances no longer dictate your activities; you begin taking responsibility for what happens in your life. Being in your own business is the difference between riding the roller coaster and being a spectator. The ride is exciting and you will want to get the most out of it.

"Shoemaker, stick to thy last." As a youngster, I heard this phrase but did not understand what it meant. I asked, "Stick to your last what?" Finally I learned that "last" meant the form used to build or repair a shoe. Then the phrase had meaning—stick with what you know.

There is a good reason that S.S.T.T.L. is important. It singles out the most valuable ingredient for success: experience. Oddly enough, it is one of the most commonly violated principles. If S.S.T.T.L. is such a good idea, why do so many deviate from it? There are a number of reasons. If you are forewarned, perhaps you will not be lured away from the path of safety.

Many people don't enjoy their work and want to get into something different. The result is that they leave fields of experience and start out anew like blind men walking through a minefield.

We also suffer from the "grass is greener on the other side of the fence" syndrome. It is not easy to make money in business, regardless how appealing it may seem from afar. What you must keep in mind is that doing well is related to experience.

Another reason to leave a field is that it is not sufficiently challenging. Or one may feel it is not a business at all. When I first went into business, I came from a background in construction. I was successful in building two houses that sold profitably. My friends were puzzled about why I did not continue this as a full-time business. I thought it was something firemen and fellows like myself did in their spare time. I couldn't have been more mistaken.

No matter how insignificant a business potential may seem, there are reasons to stick with what you know. Any business can become enormous through vertical integration or simply through multiplication. Our world is heavily populated and has an insatiable appetite for goods and services.

There are boundless opportunities within all fields, including your own, without having to switch to unknown ones. If you really seek challenge, you can find it within your own game. Vernon Rudolph was an extraordinarily gifted businessman. He needed challenge the way we all need oxygen. While he started out with one small doughnut shop, he never left his game. He expanded into new facets that became large enterprises, and all involved doughnuts. He was a shoemaker who never left his "last."

Another reason people leave what they know best is that they feel it is not prestigious enough. For years, Vernon Rudolph had difficulty recruiting top management candidates because many did not want to build a lifetime of work around doughnuts. If prestige is important to you, remember that success in business is a function of what you make out of it and not a function of what you do.

Some people will leave what they know best because they're having trouble with it, and they wish to escape. This happened to me. During a business recession, I switched to another field in which I had no experience, and the result was a total disaster. It was a hard way to learn the principle of "Shoemaker, stick to thy last."

If you were planning a long sea voyage, you surely would prepare for handling storms. There are certain things one does in storms and other things one never does. Your decisions will make the difference between capsizing or surviving. Similarly, once in business, be prepared to handle ups and downs. Without a plan, it is easier than you can imagine to do the very opposite of what you should do. When your feet are in the fire, your thinking may not be clear, and there is an instinctive desire to escape. Rather than escape into an untried field, your plans for handling business difficulties should include the doctrine of S.S.T.T.L.

Sometimes business people leave their fields of experience because they are talked into it. You would be astonished how one can be "sold" into unhappy deals. Remember, there are promoters out there who can sell shoes to people who don't have feet. They are perfectly capable of selling you a business that you have absolutely no reason to be in.

Another way we get trapped in unfamiliar businesses is through overconfidence from success in another business. My partner, Frank Watase, and I recently had lunch with an H.B.S. classmate of Frank's, Joe Lynum. Joe is an investment banker. He knows many successful men of middle age who have made their mark in businesses. Joe observed that after achieving success, many get involved in new businesses that are outside their areas of experience and suddenly find themselves losers for the first time in their lives.

There is some special allure for successful businessmen about going into the restaurant business. Wealthy entrepreneurs succumb to the notion that they are restaurant experts because they have spent so much time dining in them. All they have really seen is the tip of the iceberg. When a person is successful in his own field, the notion of running a restaurant seems as easy as falling off a log. They fall off the log, all right . . . straight into the pits.

You probably know people who *were* successful, and then failed in something they knew little about. I've seen educated, experienced business executives open doughnut shops and look pretty silly, and unfortunately, come to grief. To succeed in a business, you must have experienced it. Any business has its own special idiosyncrasies and complexities and truths. A successful person in a tough business can be lured into another that seems simple, and be devastated.

On the other hand, you also know of people who started a new business in a field they were familiar with and did well. When a CPA who has been practicing for years in a large firm decides to start his own accounting office, you can almost predict success. Think of this same person opening a doughnut shop and you can almost certainly predict failure—not because doughnuts are such a mysterious or complex business, but simply because the CPA doesn't know the ropes in that field.

The other day my IBM typewriter broke down. In looking through the yellow pages, I found my eye caught by an advertisement. It was a repair service that fixed only IBM typewriters. Naturally this ad appealed to me and I took the machine in. It turned out to be a fellow who had worked for IBM as a serviceman for eleven years and who had been on his own for seven years. He had a very good business. How could he not succeed? He was a shoemaker who even stuck to the one make of shoes he knew best.

My wife, Peggy, used to take her "Z" sports car into the local dealership for servicing. Service was so erratic, expensive, and inefficient that she won't go back. What an opportunity for a "Z" mechanic who wants to be in business! If he opened up across the street and put up a sign that said "Z service only," he would have more business than he could handle. He would also be in a safe business because he would be guided by S.S.T.T.L.

Now, let's look at a problem that faces many aspiring entrepreneurs as well as those already in business. What if you don't like what you do, and want to be in a different business? For example, let's say your experience has been in education and you now wish to start your own business. Also, let's assume you have another reason to start your own business: you don't want to teach anymore. Under these conditions it may seem impossible to apply "Shoemaker." Not so. Here is how to proceed.

You first decide, using Steps One and Two of this book, what your new business will be. It could be a far cry from teaching. Then, experience that business before going into it. *Work for someone else who is in it.* Study it long and carefully, in addition to your work experience in it. Now you are clear to proceed on your own.

A shopping center developer once offered our company a fine location for a Yum Yum Donut Shop in Camarillo, California. There was an independent doughnut shop across the street. Now, if the independent doughnut shop was a good one, our policy would be to pass the location. Two competing shops that close together would not do well.

We did have to determine, however, whether the independent was a good operator. If he was not, we would disregard him because he wouldn't be there long anyway. To find out, I arranged to meet the owner at his store. He turned out to be a man who had been a police officer for fifteen years. He left for two reasons: to get out of police work, and to fulfill his desire to have his own business. He had learned the doughnut business by working for the prior owner of the shop. He worked long enough before starting on his own to become an expert doughnut baker. He had also learned the do's and don'ts of his business before he started. He didn't deviate from what he learned.

His operation was a good one and we passed up the location across the street. We respected him because he had learned his new business well, operated it well, and he practiced S.S.T.T.L. You can switch fields of endeavor and still practice this doctrine.

Let's assume you are in a business that is your true love, but feel it is not substantial enough to be a long-range challenge. Having a business that is built around an activity you love is incredibly good fortune. Before discarding it, you should stop and analyze what possibilities you can make out of it if you really put your mind to it.

Since we have referred to "Shoemaker," let's assume you are a shoemaker working for yourself and you love what you do. Also, you don't think running a shoe shop will achieve your goals. Make a list of all the possibilities that could result from your knowledge of how to repair shoes:

1. Have a big shop with lots of employees.
2. Develop a chain of shoe repair shops.
3. Manufacture specialty shoes, like Gucci.
4. Sell supplies to other shoemakers.
5. Promote and merchandise your repair business.
6. Start a shoe-shining operation in your shop.
7. Sell shoes.
8. Import and distribute shoes.
9. Manufacture other leather goods, such as handbags
10. Sell other leather goods, such as coats.

You begin to see that being a shoemaker offers endless possibilities for those experienced in it. I recently read about a fellow named Christopher Brevidoro who loved lilacs. He started out with $1.50 and began growing them. Today he has a sixty-acre lilac ranch and supplies 90 percent of the California lilac market.

Thus, even nonbusinesslike activities can be potential opportunities. It makes a great deal of sense for you to stick with what you love to do, once you are in your own business.

Let's summarize "Shoemaker, stick to thy last":

1. S.S.T.T.L. is a characteristic trait of a winner.
2. Losers frequently violate S.S.T.T.L.
3. If you want to start a business you are inexperienced in, work for someone else first in that field.
4. Don't let success in your own business lead you to believe you can operate another business successfully.
5. Don't let business troubles cause you to switch into something else that you do not know.
6. Unlimited challenges can be found within your own business without having to go outside.
7. When you have learned and experienced a business that works, stick with it.

31

A PLEASANT EXPERIENCE

This chapter will show you how to measure success once you are in business. Many people who start a business never stop to count the scorecard. Most of us become so committed to our businesses that we give no thought at all to measuring our success. The only criterion normally considered is how much money we are making.

There is another one. Stop and decide if you're having a *pleasant experience* from two standpoints: 1. Does your business result in a pleasant experience for customers? 2. Does your business result in a pleasant experience for you?

The answers will strip away all the frivolous reasons that

keep people in business. Or these answers might verify that you are indeed achieving success.

First, decide to what degree your customers have a pleasant experience. Your answer will not only help measure your success but it will also furnish an indication of your future business stability. If your customers are not having a pleasant experience, you might later find yourself on top of a pile of nothing.

Henry Ford once said: "The only foundation of real business is service." If your customer is not well served, his experience with you will not be pleasant. Success is therefore dependent on your philosophy of doing business. If you have an underlying and unremitting goal to contribute something worth while to your customer in return for his business, then you are likely to create a pleasant experience for him.

To understand how APE (a pleasant experience) can be used to judge virtually any business situation, let me illustrate my experiences on a recent ski trip to Lake Tahoe, California. Between Christmas and the New Year, Tahoe is packed with skiers. Some months before, we had made sight-unseen reservations for this week at a motel.

The motel was everything we expected with respect to location and features. It was owned and operated by a couple with small children who had recently moved from the midwest and who were the new proprietors. Although it was fine at first glance, there were some things about the motel that made our visit something less than a pleasant experience, and I would guess that the owners were completely oblivious of the deficiencies. The heat in the bathroom was without controls. The windows onto a public balcony did not lock. An outside fluorescent light used to illuminate the building at night shone directly into the room.

Who tells the proprietor that he failed to create a pleasant experience? Certainly not the customer, because that itself is an unpleasant experience the customer can do without. The owner must determine for himself. The owner is either in business to serve or he is simply in business. This single difference separates the winners from the losers.

Did the new owners ever read a book on how to run a motel? I doubt it. Did they ever take any courses on the subject? Probably not. Were they in the business before, working for someone else? Nope. They will be like those who wander out onto the freeway and get hit by a bus.

They are going to get hit by the bus of professional competitors, and they probably won't ever know what hit them. Their competitors are specialists in achieving APE for their guests. The moment of truth does not come between Christmas and the New Year when everybody does business, but when the going gets rough. The survivors will be doing business with repeat customers who have enjoyed APE and who come back for more. The amateurs will end up with crumbs and ultimately they will starve.

The professional motels at Tahoe probably don't consider the place we stayed at as competition at all. Here's why:

1. The pros create APE for customers and the amateurs do not.
2. The pros have staying power and build sales through repeat business.
3. The pro will replace a manager who is incompetent.

Harsh stuff, but it gets to the truth in judging your success. While on the same ski trip, a fellow on a chair lift recommended a restaurant, the buffet dinner at Harrah's Hotel. We went and found a long wait. The hostess took our name and said there would be a wait of one and a half hours. We waited. We were called in one hour (pleasant) and enjoyed an incredibly good meal.

The following evening we visited a small restaurant. The hostess told us there would be a half-hour wait. After forty-five minutes we realized it was going to be much longer and so we finally left (an unpleasant experience). We walked across the street to another restaurant and had a dinner that on a scale of one to ten was about two. An inexperienced owner stood by helplessly watching the waitresses handle overloaded stations.

The next time we are in Tahoe, where do you think we will eagerly look forward to dinner? Harrah's, of course. You will surely agree that APE is an ultimate goal and also a method for evaluating your success as an entrepreneur.

People going into business cling to preconceived concepts about their new businesses. This is natural because they are entering a world they have not experienced before. Usually the reality of a new business has little in common with one's concept of it before starting. No one can describe it for you. How do you describe the experience of parachuting from a plane?

If being in your own business is going to produce a pleasant experience for you, then by all means:

1. Keep your agreements with respect to business objectives.
2. Maintain your goals regarding a balanced life.
3. Be free of worry.

Losing sight of objectives can turn pleasant experiences into horror stories. For example, if one of your objectives in starting a business is "quality without compromise," and you start purchasing cheap materials, you have lost sight of that goal.

Your own pleasant experience can be enhanced by how well balanced your life is. If you don't have time to smell the roses, you won't find business to be a pleasant experience. Life is too short not to enjoy it, and if you're not having fun, you are not successful.

You should measure your success by the presence or absence of worry. A worried existence drains you of rest and confidence. You can't lead a worried life and be successful, because you won't be happy.

Self-evaluation does not always reach the truth because we tend to defend our mistakes and accept unhappy circumstances we have created for ourselves. Look at your business from the standpoint of your customers: "Is this a pleasant experience?" Also, ask yourself as an individual: "Is it a pleasant experience being in my own business?"

If your answers to these questions are yes and you wish to press onward, then you must enhance your customer's pleasant experience by serving him better in every way you can. As for yourself, strive to maintain balance in your life by being happy and not worrying.

On the other hand, your self-evaluation may fall short when you use APE as your criterion for success. If so, you arrive at a moment of truth. You might decide to change the things in your business and life that get in the way of making business a pleasant experience. Or you might curtail the adventure of entrepreneurship and seek another avenue of earning a living. If going into business creates worry and unhappiness, it is simply not worth it.

This technique for self-evaluation can be periodically used to test your status. From time to time, ask yourself the APE questions to be sure you're happy.

32
UNBEND THE BOW

You may recall that Abraham Lincoln was harshly criticized during the Civil War for his storytelling episodes. After one lashing by the press, Lincoln disclosed to a friend that his storytelling enabled him to maintain some semblance of equilibrium in his anguished life. The way he expressed it was: "To shoot an arrow straight, one must from time to time unbend the bow." Unbending the bow is especially important when you are not inclined to do so. Starting a business is one of those times.

Being in your own business is a different way of life from working for someone else. There is one unfortunate abnormality that frequently develops. You can become eccentric. You spend too much time at work and miss out on other activities that as an employee you have taken for granted. Your life can lose its juice and flavor because work crowds out the fun.

I address this subject with a good deal of authority. Most of the pleasures of life escaped me once I started in business for myself. For years, being in my own business resulted in a rather dismal life. Going into my own business was not the mistake, it was permitting business to crowd out other activities and pleasures.

Recently I visited a business acquaintance whom I had not seen for about one year. The last time I saw him, he seemed to be hobbling a bit, although not seriously enough to warrant conversation. The latest visit was a different story. He had a strange, pale quality about him. His left arm was in a brace, and so I asked him about it with considerable uneasiness.

He told me he was suffering from what is known as "Lou Gehrig's disease," a progressive, debilitating illness for which there is presently no cure. He said he thought such afflictions always happened to someone else and he was surprised to be experiencing it himself. His conclusion was simple. He calmly looked me in the eye and said: "Life is too short not to enjoy it." Those words tell it all. Chalk that phrase up and read it every day or so. It will help remind you of the pitfall of eccentricity.

Of course, you don't have to be in business to develop an unbalanced life. The other evening I was on a flight from San Jose to Burbank, and I engaged in conversation with a businessman sitting next to me. A sharp-looking fellow about thirty-five years old, he worked for IBM and had been on an assignment in San Jose. He was married, had children, and was returning home that evening.

I asked him how long he had been away. His answer floored me: three weeks. It takes forty-five minutes to fly from San Jose to Burbank. I mentioned that three weeks seemed like a long time to be gone, and his answer was, "Well, I try to get ahead, so I have been working through the weekends." Now, that's eccentric. Get ahead of what? His work got ahead of his family, his children, his pleasures, and all of the other parts of his life that deserve care and time.

The risk of becoming eccentric is greater in some occupations than others. The office of President of the United States is a good example of high risk for a badly balanced life. Franklin Roosevelt was absolutely burned out physically, emotionally, and intellectually at the age of sixty-two. Through work, through worry, and without compensating balances of exercise, rest and leisure, F.D.R. suffered a severe loss of effectualness and finally a premature death.

A person starting in business is especially vulnerable to eccentricity. Since the experience is new, there will be doubts and fears. Also, having your savings at stake tends to make you spend too much time at business. To avoid an unhappy and irregular existence, I have a plan for you.

Structure your activities around a master plan that will make your life full and happy. Life is a celebration to enjoy and to share with others. Work alone will not produce happiness. Neither will any other single activity. Together, in balance and in harmony, a group of activities can produce the good life.

To develop your own master plan, start by making a list of activities you want in your life. You have to decide if this list is to be developed by yourself or if you want your wife or family to participate. As shown in the following sample master plan, make your own commitments as to how you plan to fulfill each desired activity. Begin to appreciate that your business is only one element in an overall combination of goals to achieve the good life.

MASTER PLAN

Activity	How to Satisfy	Time
Family	Time with spouse and children Dinnertime	Every day
Business	Work intensively	Monday-Friday 8 A.M.-6 P.M.
Avocation	Write	6 hours/week
Exercise	Run (also avocation)	5 times/week 3 miles
Vacations	Camping, travel	1 week in winter, 4 weeks in summer
Worship	Church	Every week
Private time	Read	1 hour/evening
Celebrate	Wine, good food, friends	Every day

This approach suggests that the answer lies in developing a plan not only for your business but also for an overall way of life that will become part of your new entrepreneurial existence. Having a plan for your life-style will prevent your work from interfering with other aspects of it. Work is only one element in your master plan, and the risk of becoming eccentric in work is neutralized.

There are certain activities that are especially important to the entrepreneur. One is avocation, "a subordinate occupation pursued in addition to one's vocation, especially for enjoyment." The work-life of the entrepreneur is normally at a level of intensity that far exceeds that of an employee. This intensity is prone to spill over into segments of the entrepreneur's life that have nothing to do with work You will take your work to bed with you, and it will occupy other waking hours.

Without an avocation, therefore, a mental vacuum can develop in nonworking hours. An avocation fills this vacuum and helps to keep work thoughts in their own time frame.

For an avocation to accomplish this, it must require complete participation. In other words, watching TV is not an avocation. Surely, flying a plane is a good one. There is no way you can be concerned about business while flying. Let's look at some other possible avocations:

    Skiing   Running
    Tennis   Gardening
    Furniture refinishing   Sailing

All of these will unbend the bow. Skiing and tennis are relatively poor ones because you cannot engage in them every day. The list could go on, and the key ingredients are participation and the ability to drop into the activity frequently and easily. My personal avocation, in addition to writing, is running. I have always admired those who have intensive avocational interests. For example, it is a blessing to be hooked on an activity such as painting. Another activity that obviously demands attention is business. The issue is how much time you will spend at it. I have some suggestions.

If your business is conducted in normal hours, have an agreement that your business week will be Monday through Friday and your nonbusiness week will be Saturday and Sunday. This agreement will be the cornerstone of your policy to avoid eccentricity. Keep Saturday and Sunday out of your business life, and do your business in five days. In Southern California there is a company called the "Four Day Tire Store." They are open only four days of the week, Thursday through Sunday. They operate just fine during those four days (which are the most important for their business) and they have three days a week to go fishing. Perhaps you can do just fine, too, by devoting five days a week to your business.

Other businesses are not conducted during normal hours. Our doughnut shop managers are responsible for stores that are open twenty-four hours, every day of the year. Also, the main thrust of our business is on weekends. The greatest problem we have with a manager is that he will burn himself out. Because of the long (virtually continuous) business hours, our managers have a much more difficult time maintaining equilibrium between work and other activities.

There was a time when I felt compelled to be the first to arrive at work and the last to leave. By my example, I was trying to show employees the virtue of hard work. I no longer have this compulsion. Employees work just as hard, or harder, if they are given authority and responsibility rather than the example of "anything you can do I can do longer."

Hard work is not necessarily a function of long hours. I have worked long hours and become too punchy to be effective, and becoming a zombie is counterproductive to the goal of business success! My own solution has evolved to a practice of limiting the days that I work to five and conducting work within certain hours of those days. I work intensively during those periods. I am much more effective, accomplish far more, and complete many more projects than I did when I worked as an entrepreneurial zombie.

For years Dr. Jim Dooley repeated one concern to me: I never took a meaningful vacation. He wasn't concerned about my pleasures; he was thinking of my health and my well-being. I recovered from the stupid eccentricity of not taking vacations. This is another way to give responsibility to employees. When you leave the business in the hands of your key employees, you can get away and return refreshed. You may even have the disquieting feeling that things ran better when you were gone than they did before you left.

You will never recapture a missed vacation. On the other hand, vacations can become the most treasured memories of your life. They should be part of your life plan, and become a legacy your family will never forget. Vacations should be scheduled every year, and I am referring to the get-out-of-town kind which is at least two weeks long, preferably longer. I look back on too many summers that were preoccupied with work and lost to myself and my family.

There are times when it is just not possible to limit work hours as much as you would like. The start-up period of a business is such a time; there are others when you have seasonal or unusual projects that just must be done. These unusual periods make it all the more important for you to maintain a proper balance between work and play during normal periods.

Don't spoil work by eccentricity, as an alcoholic spoils the pleasure of wine by overindulgence. Nothing, nothing is worth becoming abnormal and self-defeating over. If being in business brings problems, let them all be real ones to be handled in your business life. Business is not a ticket to a self-created hell. If you cannot handle your life sensibly while running your own business, you must remember that the price is paid by your family as well as by yourself. You can always work for someone else and enjoy life.

The key, then, to really successful business ownership is to go in with an overall plan that includes time for work and for all the other parts of your life. Keep in mind:

1. Have an avocation.
2. Limit your work hours.
3. Take vacations.

Success in this overall approach will enrich your life. Remember, it is too short not to enjoy.

33
STAY WELL

On July 29, 1979, the U.S. Surgeon General issued a report that was remarkable. It did not receive widespread publicity yet it was as important as the 1964 Surgeon General's *Report on Smoking and Health*. The new report stated that Americans must start a second public health revolution: one to *prevent* all disease, similar to the first health revolution at the turn of the century that attacked infectious disease.

The 1979 report called on Americans to make momentous adjustments in their diet and habits to reduce their death rate by 20 percent to 35 percent in various age groups by 1990. To do so, the report said, people must cut their intake of alcohol, salt, sugar, and fats, especially saturated fats.

The Surgeon General cited an analysis estimating that as many as half of American deaths in 1976 were attributed to unhealthy behavior or life-styles. He declared, "Prevention is an idea whose time has come." Among the report's points:

- **a.** Cigarette smoking is the principal preventable cause of chronic disease and death in this country.
- **b.** Alcohol is a factor in more than 10 percent of all deaths in the United States.
- **c.** Personal life-styles are responsible for a large share of unnecessary disease and disability in the United States.

The report represents an important consensus among doctors and medical scientists. A time has been reached, they say, when people can do far more to improve their health by acting themselves than they can by waiting for symptoms and then going to doctors.

We see evidence of this report everywhere. I like to watch

people in airports. Most of my air travel is between southern California and northern California on flights that are primarily for business people. Waiting for planes can be interesting when you are watching others waiting for them. I see all sizes and shapes: some look great and others look gross. Some are obviously fit and others have the unmistakable signs of the unhealthy life-style referred to by the Surgeon General. For the entrepreneur, the difference is crucial.

To illustrate the difference between being well and being the victim of unhealthy behavior, let's look at show business. Actors seem to gravitate toward one of two extremes. At one extreme are those who stay well and take extraordinary care to protect and enhance their image. Others lead notoriously self-destructive lives. You surely have seen actors who were stars a decade ago suddenly resurface in TV parts looking incredibly, devastatingly aged. I suppose the single greatest implement used to accomplish this physical unraveling is booze.

Entrepreneurs react in the same way as people in show business do. Some use their success as an incentive to stay well, others use it as an excuse to start a self-destructive life-style. Entrepreneurship is best approached as the opportunity for a healthy and disciplined life-style. As you learn more of the implications of going into your own business, you realize it encompasses an overall philosophy of life. You begin to see that your life can broaden into entirely new horizons of

1. Achievement
2. Discipline
3. Contribution
4. Faith
5. Risk
6. Reward
7. Well-being

An entrepreneur's life becomes a new life, rather than just a new business. It is a life that is more intense and a great deal fuller. This philosophy demands the enhancement of physical and mental well-being so that you will achieve success in your overall life plan as a business person.

Like an athlete who must be conditioned in order to win, the businessman must be well and strong. In your business the buck stops with you. You cannot afford to be physically and mentally impaired. My father tried to get into business late in life and was doomed before he started because he did not have physical health. Becoming an entrepreneur is like getting into the big leagues; you had better be in condition.

How do you stay well? As the Surgeon General has reported, you do so by preventing disease. The way to do this has already been determined by the Human Population Laboratory of the California State Department of Health in Berkeley. They spent more than ten years studying the life habits and resulting health of 7000 adults in Alameda County. They came to the conclusion that there are seven factors with significance for longevity and well-being, and if a forty-five-year-old man practices six of these habits he can expect to live eleven years longer than a man of the same age who observes fewer than three. His life expectancy will expand from sixty-seven years to seventy-eight years. More impressive still, a man fifty-five to sixty-four years old who has observed all seven habits will have the same physical condition as a man of twenty-five to thirty-four who has observed zero to two. Here are the seven habits:

1. Have meals at regular times; no snacking.
2. Have breakfast regularly.
3. Maintain moderate weight.
4. Don't smoke.
5. Drink moderately, if at all.
6. Get adequate sleep: seven or eight hours a night.
7. Exercise moderately to briskly two to three times a week.

There are enormous differences in older people, both physically and in mental capacity. Some are still going strong at eighty-five and others are ready to check out at sixty. To a large measure our longevity depends upon our parents, and since we cannot control this factor, we must control those things that can be manipulated to achieve well-being and a long life.

Old people who exist as vegetables have in many cases contributed to their unfortunate state by their habits over the years. Those who maintain health have earned it by leading lives of common sense and prudence. The entrepreneur has a special reason to stay well. He not only has a business to run but also a life-style to enhance.

Work itself never seems to be a reason for loss of vitality. On the contrary, those who never retire from work seem to do the best of all. The TV news had an interview recently with a gravedigger who has dug over 600 graves for his present employer and still has no thought of quitting, at the age of ninety-three.

If you are going to stay well, you will have to train for it. A professional athlete makes training a part of his life because his success depends on his physical condition. If you really think about it, the entrepreneur is in exactly the same position as the athlete. He must also keep in condition and stay well, because his success depends on it.

Aside from the importance to your business, staying well has other benefits. You gain a sense of power that is exhilarating, you lenghten your life-span and add quality and zest to your daily life, and you enhance your sex life.

Starting your own business is going to be one of the great adventures of your life. Up to this point you may never have had the opportunity to fully exercise your maximum capabilities. You will need stamina to perform at your best, so you must stay well physically. To implant the "seven keys to staying well" as your standard life-style, consider a simple daily self-examination. Type up the seven items on a small card and put it in a conspicuous but private place, such as the mirror of your bedroom. At the start of each day, chart the course. Live in a way that will keep you well.

34

VAYA CON DIOS

There is an interesting collection of famous last words of notable people that includes two entrepreneurs. One was P.T. Barnum and the other was an unnamed owner of a chain of restaurants. The final words of Barnum were, "What were the receipts today?" The last request of the restaurant tycoon was: "Tell them to slice the ham a little thinner."

Surely the ultimate goal of the entrepreneur must be more than the wish to have the ham sliced thinner. The final unanswered question must be more important than today's receipts.

Once during a stockholder's meeting of Polaroid Corporation, chairman Edwin Land had gone into a discourse on the goals of the corporation. A stockholder finally asked, "Yes, but what is the bottom line of all of this?" After a thoughtful pause, Mr. Land's reply was: "Well, the real bottom line is heaven."

One interpretation of what Edwin Land calls heaven is described in a story my friend Philip Anderson tells about a man who was granted an opportunity to see what heaven and hell were like. He decided to take a look at hell first, and was taken into a huge cave where a gigantic table had been set. Every imaginable delicacy was spread out, and it looked like the greatest smorgasbord of all time. Around this banquet table were seated an endless array of people, all of whom had three-foot long spoons strapped to their arms. The spoons were so long they could not put the food into their mouths. It was a frustrating, wretched scene.

The man was then taken to see what heaven was like. He saw an identical table with the same incredible feast prepared for a huge throng. Everyone seated around this banquet table also had long spoons strapped to their arms, but the scene was entirely different. They were all having a marvelous time. The difference was that they were all serving each other.

Serving others can be a problem for the entrepreneur. He faces an ironic paradox: the more he succeeds in business the less he is inclined to serve. Serving others will be crowded out by "the attractions of this world and the delights of wealth, and the search for success and lure of nice things."

Yet the entrepreneur has many opportunities to serve others that can be realized within his business and also in outside philanthropy. An associate of mine, Bob Meadows, made a complete change in the crew of a high-volume doughnut shop by hiring people who all had recently been released from prison. They were felony offenders who were unable to find jobs because of their records, and Bob provided them with a means of rejoining the world again. For himself, Bob enjoyed a rewarding experience.

The final measure of success in your own business will be how you handle the entrepreneur's paradox (or should we say curse), which is to forget about serving others. You overcome this by expanding your comprehensive entrepreneurial goal to include service to others. You may not be able to solve the big problems of the human race, but if you can't then perhaps you can feed some of the abandoned children or help with others to collectively cure the leukemias of this world. If the bottom line of being in your own business makes sense within the eternal scope of things, then it becomes a worthwhile goal indeed.

Entrepreneurs are an unusual breed, and in addition to the desire to control their own lives and set their own goals, they have another trait, which is faith; "The confident assurance that something we want is going to happen. It is the certainty that what we hope for is waiting for us, even though we cannot see it up ahead." Faith in your overall goals will keep you plowing a furrow that is straight, and the hardships that you encounter in business will act as strengthening and stabilizing influences in your life. Your posture will become one of supreme confidence, and the means of escape from senseless worry.

If you are a person who fits the true mold of "entrepreneur," no discouragements will keep you from achieving your goal. For those of you who do undertake this exciting adventure, I can only say, finally, *"Vaya con Dios."*

INDEX

Abbey Rents, 79
Abbey Rents and Sells, 79
Abdul-Jabbar, Kareem (Lew Alcindor), 39
Accountants, 118, 129, 197, 222
  fees of, 187
  pricing policy and, 208
  problems and, 215
  purchases and, 189
  use of, from start, 126, 127
Accounting, 125–30
  cash flow as defined in, 132; *see also* Cash flow
Ackles, Virgil, 91–93
Activities
  lists of activities enjoyed, 56
  See also Work
Actual cash flow, 137
Advertising, 201–2, 206, 207
  word-of-mouth, 105, 108
Advice, seeking, 28, 29
Akre, Ethel, 211
Akre, Rudy, 211
Amigos restaurants, 114, 115
Anderson, Bob, 72, 73
Anderson, Philip, 240
Associated Hosts, 78, 79
Athletes, champion, 37–41
Attorneys, *see* Lawyers

Audits, 127
  annual, and loans, 197
Authority
  partnership and, 88
  to sign checks, 128
Avocation, 232–33, 235

Backup sources, 187
Balance, cash flow, *see* Cash-flow control
Balance sheet, 126
  ratios in, 130
Bankruptcy, 150–53
  loans and prior, 199
Bankers (and banks), 118
  accounting and, 128, 130
  borrowing from, 193–99
  cash flow, capital expenses and, 137, 139
  cash flow control and, 139
  forecast balance and, 136
  franchise and, 123
  problems and, 215
Barbers, 70
Barnum, P. T., 240
Basic needs, businesses filling, 62
Baskin-Robbins, 89

Be-do-have sequence, 33–34
Bidders, 186
Boethings Nursery, 107
Bombay Bicycle Club, 78
Bonding of construction work, 189
Bonus, manager, *see* Profit centers
Bookkeeping, 125–28
   See also Accountants; Accounting
Botello, Wally, 105
Brains
   as ingredient for success, 35–37, 47
   test of, 48
Bread trucks, home delivery, 71
Brevidoro, Christopher, 224
Brookdale Ice Cream Company, 78
Brooks Brothers, 89
Budgets, operating, 128
Bulasky, Joe, 78–79
Business
   art of, 82
   See also specific subjects; for example: Decisions; Leases; Problems
Business administration, 116–17
Business failures
   characteristics of, 62
   See also Bankruptcy
"Business opportunities" section of newspapers, 25

Callender, Marie, 106
Capital
   determining, needed for start-up, 140
   and fixed assets, 198
   as ingredient for success, 35–36, 47
   other people's, 192–93
   and profit-center plans, 174
   sources of, *see* Loans; *and specific sources*
   test of, 48
Capital expenses, cash flow and, 137, 139
Car dealerships, 121
Cars, 71, 70
Carter, Jimmy, 210
Case histories
   of bankruptcy, 150–53
   of cash-flow control, 139
   of dedication, 44–45
   of entrepreneur's instinct, 31–33
   of filling a need, 63
   of learning by doing, 99
   of life-span of business, 67, 70–72
   of pilot operation, 112–14
   of pleasant experience, 226–28
   of quality without compromise, 102–8
   of specialization, 77–81
   of traits of bad business people, 144–49
   of traits of good business people, 141–44, 149
   of work loved, 54–55
Cash flow, 126
   borrowing and, 198–99
   problems from inadequate, 209, 213
   purchases and, 191
   and taxes, 128
Cash-flow control, 130–40
   checklist of "out" items for, 135
   long-range, table, 138
   table, 133
Celebrity identification, 206
Certified financial statements, 127–28, 197
Certified Public Accountant (CPA), *see* Accountants
Chain operation, testing before starting a. 109

Chasen, Dave, 99–100
Chasen's, 99–100
Checks
  and cash flow control, 137
  signing, 128
Clayton, Derek, 41
Coaches, winning, 38–40
Coca Cola Bottling Co.,
    franchising by, 121
Coffee Dan's, 79
Colonel Sanders' chicken, 103
Commercial properties, leasing,
    166; *see also* Leases
Communication
  of complaints, 190
  between partners, 96
  by professionals, 118
Competition
  in business, 43
  as catalyst of free enterprise,
      200
  customers and existing, 62–63
  and filling a need, 66
  location and, 161–63; *see also*
      Location
  and pricing, 208
  quality without compromise
      and, 101
Competitiveness of winners, 41
Complaints, communicating, 190
Computerized bookkeeping, 127
Concepts, pilot operations and,
    111, 112, 115
Concessions, 188
Construction work, bonding, 189
Contingencies
  buying subject to, 190
  in lease, 168
Control
  checks as means of, 128
  of dishonesty, 129
  franchise and loss of, 122, 123
  internal, 127
  inventory, 183, 184

  See also Cash-flow control
Convenience market, small, 73
Cooling-off period, 67
Corporate life, 32
Corporation
  as better business form, 88
  selling stock in, 193
Corvettes (cars), 80, 144
Cost-of-living clause, 168
Costs, *see specific types of costs*
Coupling cards, 55, 58–60
Credibility
  loans and, 199
  selling, to lender, 196
Credit, small start-up and, 36
Criticism between partners, 97

Debt, 193
Decision-making tests, 27–29
Decisions
  cards to assist in, 55–61
  for oneself, 46–50
  prudence in, 35
  thought necessary to, 23–29
  on type of business, 81–84, 116,
      117
Decor, use of professional, 205
Dedication, 44–48
  test of, 48
  of winners, 41
Demonstrations, 206
Denny's, 120, 122
Direct selling, 71
Discipline
  to preserve success, 42–43
  of winners, 41
  See also Work
Discount department stores, 115
Dishonesty, 129
Displays, 206
Dog House, The, 113
Dooley, Jim, 234

Drew Theological Seminary, 209

Eccentricity, as risk, 230–31
Ecclesiastes, as source of philosophy, 53
Edsel (car), 113
Education
  in accounting, 125, 126
  in management, 116–19
  See also Training
Eisenhower, Dwight D., 140, 154, 155, 159
Employee benefit package, 130
Endurance of winners, 42
Energy, 40
Energy costs, 72
Enjoyment of work, *see* Work
Enthusiasm, calculated thought and, 27
Entrepreneurs
  definition of, 30
  traits of, 46–50
  traits of, tested, 42, 48–49
Entrepreneur's instinct, 30–33, 35–37, 47
  test of, 48
Exaggeration in asking for loans, 195–96
Exhibits, 170
Expanding needs, businesses filling, 62
Expansion, risking, 152
Experience
  in accounting, 126
  acquiring, 116–18
  on how to buy, 183–84
  pleasant, as success, 225–29
  before plunging in, 153
  and profit-center plans, 174
  risk and lack of management, 152
  and sticking to what you know, 219–25
  See also Know-how; Training
Extras, approved in writing, 189

Family, 27
Favorite-activity cards, 55, 56, 60
Favorite-senses cards, 55–57, 60
Financial report, 126
Financial statements, 125–30
  certified, 127–28, 197
Financing, *see* Capital; *and specific sources of financing; for example;* Bankers; Suppliers
Fitzpatrick, Peggy (Peggy Holland), 38, 107, 44, 222
Fixed assets, 198
Fixed costs, 202
Food operations, 73, 78–79
"For" and "against" lists
  in decision making, 28, 29, 48, 49
  evaluating partnership with, 90–91
Ford, Henry, 33, 64, 226
Ford Motor Company, 113
Forecast bank balance, 136
Fortune (magazine), 82, 100
Four Day Tire Store, 233
Franchising, 113, 119–25, 151
Free enterprise system, 200
Freud, Sigmund, 53
Funds, misuse of, 129

Games, winning, 37–43
Garfinkle, Ben, 94, 95, 139
General Motors, 121
Getty, J. Paul, 33, 88
Goal(s), 228

liking one's work as basic, 53
Goal-oriented dedication, 44-46
Graduate business schools, 117
Graduate school training, 117-19
Grocery stores, 73
   life-span of, 68, 69
Guts
   as ingredient for success, 30-33, 35-37, 47
   quality without compromise and, 106
   test of, 48

Haney, Ellie, 38
Haney, Terry, 38
Hard work, 45-46, 92, 234
   See also Work
Hardware stores, 73
Harrah's Hotel, 227, 228
Harvard Business School, 32, 92, 116, 118, 221
Haste, as enemy of pilot operations, 110-12, 114
Health, 72, 237-39
Health insurance, 130
High-risk undertaking, committing resources to, 28
Hirsch, Joe, 141-42
Hirsch Pipe and Supply Company, 141, 142
Hitchcock, Alfred, 77
Hobbies, 55
Holland, Jamie, 94
Holland, Peggy, 38, 107, 144, 222
Holland Construction Company, 92
Hughes, Howard, 88
Hula Hoop, 68, 69

Impatience, thinking and, 26

Impetuosity, 35
Improvements, 197
Incentive pay, 175
   leveraged profit-sharing as, 175-79
   See also Profit centers
Income level, location and, 161
Income statement, weekly, 127
Income taxes, 128
Inspiration, 39, 40
Instructions, willingness to follow, of winners, 40
Insurance, health, 130
Internal Revenue Service, 129
International Industries, 113
Inventory control, 183, 184
Investment banking, 70

Joan of Arc, 209
Johns-Manville Corporation, 31-32, 74, 91, 141
Julie's Place, 78

K-Mart, 115
Kaiser, Henry, 33
Kennedy, John F., 30-31
Know-how
   acquiring, *see* Case histories
   development of, 141
   and franchising, 119-21, 123
   as ingredient for success, 35-37
   and small start-up, 36
   winner's, 38, 39
   See also Experience; Training
Knowledge
   before starting, 44-45
   See also Education; Know-how; Learning
Kresge, 115

Krispy Kreme Doughnut
  Corporation, 142, 143

Labor costs, 129
Labor savings, 72
Land, Edwin, 240
Landlords, 166–73, 197
  approvals by, 170
Lawyers, 118
  and employee dishonesty, 129
  fees of, 187
  and lease, 167
  need for, 95
  and problems, 215
  value of, 91–92
Lawry's Prime Rib Restaurant, 79
Learning
  ability for, of winners, 40
  by doing, 98–100
  fear of, 26–27
  to handle problems, *see*
    Problems
  from others, 141–53; *see also*
    Case histories
  to sell, 204
  test of ability for, 42
Leasehold improvements, 169, 171
Leases, 166–73
  checklist of issues involving,
    167–73
  negotiating, 166–73
Leasing companies, 196
Leisure time, 71
Lever Brothers, 89
Leverage, 192, 198
Leveraged profit-sharing plan,
    175–79
Liabilities of partners, 88
Life insurance on partners, 95
Life span of business, 67–70
  graph illustrating, 68
  long, 73
  ups and downs and, 69–70
Lights, 205–6
Lincoln, Abraham, 111, 229–30
Liquidity, 131–32
  and purchases, 184
  See also Cash-flow control
Litmus paper test of partnership,
    87, 89–90
Loans, 192–200
  cash flow and, 137, 139
  sources of, 195–97
Location
  checklist on, 81–84, 164
  choosing, 159–65
  criteria for choosing, 161–62
  need and, 65–66
  negotiating lease for, *see* Leases
Long-term lease, 167
Long-term loans, 197
Los Angeles Times (newspaper),
    92
Loses, reducing, 210–11
Love
  of activity, 40; *see also* Work
  between partners, 97
Lynum, Joe, 221

McDonald's, 75, 104, 116, 120,
    122
McGannis, Tom, 102–3
Maintenance costs, 128
Management, fundamentals of,
    116–19
Manager bonus system, 127
  See also Profit centers
Managers, 234
  as key to large business, 173
  professional, 99, 100, 106–7
  See also Profit centers
Manufacturing, test operation for,
    109
Marie Callender Pies, 106

Master plan for life, 231-32
Maturing of thought, 27, 28
Max Factor, 113
Meadows, Bob, 241
Merchandising, 200-8
  costs, 202-3
  and high volume, 202-3
  pointers on, 204-7
Microdot, 64
Midas, 77
Milne, Frank, 54, 80, 144
Mind, state of, 39
Moderation to preserve success, 42-43
Money
  borrowing, see Loans
  as enemy of pilot operation, 111, 112, 114-15
  franchising and, 119-25
  liquidity and, 132
  and professionals, 118; see also Profit centers
  See also Capital
Moreno, Hank, 31, 32, 34
Motivation, 39, 40
Multiple-unit business, 112

National Donut Corporation, 91, 92
Natural ability
  test of, 42
  of winners, 40, 41
Needs
  changing business for filling, 73-74
  examples of, 65
  filling, 61-66
Neville, Jeanne Haney, 38
Newsstands, 170

Objectivity in decision making, 29

Olympic Games (1976), 38
O.P.M. (other people's money), 192-93
Ownership
  dilution of, in partnership, 88
  profit-center managers and, 175
  rewards of, 31

Packaging, 206
Parking rights, 169
Partnerships (and partners), 87-97
  as business form, 88
  guidelines for choosing, 95-96
  risking, 152
  successful, 89-90, 92-95
  unsuccessful, 91-92
Paul of Tarsus, 97
Payment
  late, 212
  loan, 195
  on time, 184-85
  after verification, 189
Percentage rent, 167-68
Percentages, critical or key, 129
Personal guarantees, 169-70
Philosophy, 53
Physical fitness, 214
Pillsbury Company, 25, 92
Pilot operations, 108-16
  energies list of, 110-12
Pleasant experience, success as, 225-29
Polaroid Corporation, 240
Ponderosa, 78
Population, location and, 162
Prevention, health and, 236
Price
  knowing, in advance, 187
  policy on, 208
  protection of, 185-86
Priorities, starting a business and life, 27

Problems, 209–16
  do's and don'ts checklist,
    211–16
  principles in handling, 210–11,
    215
Product
  confidence in, as enemy of pilot
    operations, 110, 112
  as key to successful selling, 201
  proprietary, as enemy of test
    operation, 111–12, 115
Profit centers, 173–82
  do's and don'ts in creating,
    180–82
  leveraged profit-sharing and,
    175–79
  nonleveraged incentive for, 179
  purpose of, 174, 175
Profit and loss (P&L) statements,
  125–30
  and profit sharing, 175–79
Profit sharing, 175–79
Profits, problems from
  inadequate, 209
Projected cash-flow, 136–37
Promises
  keeping, 212–13
  in writing, 189
Prudence, importance of, 35
Publicity, 206
Purchase orders in writing, 186
Purchases, 129, 183–91

Quality without compromise
  (QWC), 100–8

Raw materials, use of best, 101
R & B Development Company, 77
Real estate, 78, 80–81
Recessions, 153

Reciprocal remedies, 170
Recognition
  of managers, 180–81
  See also Profit centers
Recourse financing, 196
Rent
  judging location on basis of, 160
  location and, 165
  percentage, 167–68
  See also Leases
Repair services, 73
Report on Smoking and Health
  (Surgeon General), 236
Reward motivation
  for managers, 175
  See also Profit centers
Rhodes, Lloyd, 54
Risk
  in borrowing money, 192
  calculation of, in decision
    making, 27–29
  of eccentricity, 230–31
  pilot operation to reduce,
    108–16
  prudence and, 35
  savings and, 151–53
  specialization reducing, 75–76
  start-up as greatest, 154–56; *see
    also* Start-up
Rock Cork, 74
Rockefeller, John D., 33, 64
Romancing suppliers, 190
Roosevelt, Franklin D., 231
Rudolph, Vernon, 142–44, 220
Runner's World (magazine), 72
Rytich, Dallas, 54

Sales, 134, 200–8, 206
Salesperson, 204
Sam's Cafe, 105
Sanders, Colonel, 103
Sara Lee, 104–5

Savings, risk and, 151–53
Scheib, Earl, 115
Schweitzer, Albert, 54–55
Sears Roebuck, 89
Security, 192
See, Mrs., 102, 115
See's Candies, 102
Selection, *see* Decisions; Location
Self-confidence
   as enemy of pilot operations, 110, 112, 114
   thinking and, 26
Self-evaluation, 46–50, 229
   tests of, 42, 48–49
Self-knowledge, 29–34
Self-sacrifice to preserve success, 42–43
Serve-people cards, 55, 57–58, 60
Service business
   quality without compromise and, 107
   test operation for, 109
Seven-Eleven stores (7-11 stores), 73
Shoemaker, stick to thy last (S.S.T.T.L.), 219–25
Short-term leases, 167
Short-term loans, 195, 197
Sight, favorite, 56, 57
Signs, 168
   importance of, 205
Silly ads, 207
Silvers, Bob, 94, 95, 139
Smell, favorite, 56, 57
Smugglers Inn, 78
Solomon (Hebrew king), 29, 53, 77, 97
Sound, favorite, 56, 57
Southland Corporation of Texas, 73
Special requirements of tenant, 170
Specialization, 75–81
   rating, 76–77

Specifications in writing, 187
Sports Chalet, 62
Standards, winner's, 38–39
Start-up, 154–56
   checklist on planning, 155–56
   location and, *see* Location
   small, 36
Steam locomotives, 68, 69, 71, 73
Stock, 192, 193
Style, role of, 113–14
Subletting, 168–69
Success
   ingredients of, 35–37
   measuring, 225–29
   prior, as enemy of pilot operations, 111, 112, 115
Senses, selling the, 205
Supermarkets, 71, 73
Suppliers
   financing from, 196
   See also Purchases
Sweat equity, 36

Taste, favorite, 56, 57
Taxes
   cash flow and, 134
   income, 128
   misuse of, 129
Telephone expenses, 128
Term discounts, 185
Test marketing, 109
Tests, *see specific tests*
Thinking, 23–29, 47
   in deciding on field of work, 54
   test of, 48
   See also Decisions
Time
   for making decisions, 27, 28
   paying bills on, 184–85
Time limit for acceptance of lease, 171
Timing, 67–74

in borrowing, 197–98
Touch, favorite, 56, 57
Traffic, location and, 161
Training
  graduate school, 117–19
  sales force, 207
  of winners, 41
  See also Education; Know-how
Training ability, test of, 42
Transite pipe, 141, 142
Tune-up Masters, 80, 81
Tunnel Vision, thinking and, 26

U.C.L.A. (University of California at Los Angeles), 38
Upham, Samuel, 209
U.S.C. (University of Southern California), 38

Vacation, 234–35
Velvet Turtle, 105
Verification, payment after, 187

Watase, Frank, 92–95, 118, 174, 194, 196, 221
Watch repairing, 71

Wells Fargo Bank, 199
What and where checklist, *see* Location
Wichell Donuts, 120
Win
  playing to, 39–41, 47
  test of, 42, 48
Winners, ingredients making, 37–43
Wives, working, 71
Wooden, John, 38–40
Word-of-mouth advertising, 105, 108
Work
  changing, 220, 223
  hard, 45–46, 92, 234
  liking, as goal, 53–54
  limiting hours of, 234, 235
  and loss of vitality, 239
  sticking to line of, 219–25
Worry, being free of, 228, 229
Wrigley, Philip, 105–6
Wrigley gum, 105

Yum Yum Donut Shops, 36, 54, 63, 92–95, 102, 121, 163, 196, 199, 205, 223

Xerox, 64